Essays in Hindu Theology

Essays in Hindu Theology

Anantanand Rambachan

FORTRESS PRESS
MINNEAPOLIS

ESSAYS IN HINDU THEOLOGY

Paperback ISBN: 978-1-5064-5312-5

eBook ISBN: 978-1-5064-5313-2

Cover image: iStock ©2019; Hand drawn decorative mandala by ekmelica

Cover design: Alisha Lofgren

For our granddaughters,
Aadyaa and Amiyaa,
with the blessing that they grow up in a world
in which all children flourish and realize
their full potential

ACKNOWLEDGMENTS

I am grateful to Saint Olaf College for granting me leave from my teaching to focus on this work. My family and my friends of all religions have been tremendous sources of support and encouragement. I am thankful to Dr. Jesudas Athyal of Fortress Press for his generous confidence in my work, to Mr. B. Parthiban for his efficient management of the production process and to Mrs. Selena George for her diligent copy-editing.

CONTENTS

ABBREVIATIONS

AU	*Aitareya Upaniṣad*
BG	*Bhagavadgītā*
BU	*Bṛhadāraṇyaka Upaniṣad*
BS	*Brahmasūtra*
CU	*Chāndogya Upaniṣad*
CW	The Complete Works of Swami Vivekananda
ĪU	*Īśa Upaniṣad*
KaU	*Kaṭha Upaniṣad*
KeU	*Kena Upaniṣad*
MāU	*Māṇḍūkya Upaniṣad*
MU	*Muṇḍaka Upaniṣad*
PU	*Praśna Upaniṣad*
ŚvU	*Śvetāśvatara Upaniṣad*
TU	*Taittirīya Upaniṣad*

The letters Bh added to the abbreviations of any text (as BSBh) indicate the commentary (*bhāṣya*) of Śaṅkara. I have also included the page numbers for ease of location.

INTRODUCTION

The essays in this volume represent three significant areas of interest to me as a Hindu scholar: critical clarification of Hindu teaching, interreligious dialogue, and liberation thought. Although I categorize the first three essays as theological, the fact is that I regard all the essays in this volume as theological in nature.

For the purpose of understanding my comfort with describing my essays as theological, I cite Frank Clooney's description of theology as "a mode of inquiry that engages a wide range of issues with full intellectual force, but ordinarily does so within the constraints of a commitment to a religious community, respect for its scriptures, traditions and practices, and a willingness to affirm the truths and values of that tradition."[1] The commitment cited here by Clooney as intrinsic to the work of the theologian, is referred to in the Hindu tradition as *śraddhā*. It is the openness to seeing the scripture as a source of valid knowledge (*pramāṇa*) and the willingness to rationally understand its claims by the employment of supportive forms of reasoning (*śāstra anukūla tarka*) that do not conflict with the disclosures of other sources of knowledge. It is this inquiring commitment or *śraddhā* that underlies and distinguishes the work of the theologian.[2]

In the case of the Hindu tradition, the inquiry that Clooney associates with the theological method, is conducted primarily into those sacred texts regarded as sources of valid knowledge (*pramāṇa*). For the Vedānta traditions, these include the *Upaniṣads*, the *Bhagavadgītā* and the *Brahmasūtras*. Specific traditions amplify this corpus. Theologians like Śaṅkara and Rāmānuja aimed to resolve internal inconsistencies in the authoritative source of knowledge and to demonstrate that it does not contradict knowledge derived from other valid sources. They offered rational expositions and understanding of sacred teachings. They exemplified a willingness, in Clooney's words, "to affirm the truths and values" of the tradition.

Hindu theology developed and flourished, when scripture was regarded as a valid source of knowledge. Sophisticated exegetical methods were developed to arrive at right meaning. Doctrinal differences were treated very seriously, carefully outlined and engaged. Reason had an important role in deciding among interpretations, reconciling conflicting passages, and in demonstrating that the claims of the *pramāṇa* are not inconsistent with what we know about the world and ourselves from other *pramāṇas*. There was an appreciation for scriptural scholarship. When scripture is no longer seen as a *pramāṇa*, however, its study, exegesis and interpretation are not very important. The intellectual disciplines that aid interpretation are also less valued.[3]

The decline of a vigorous exegetical tradition in contemporary Hinduism, is one of the reasons, I believe, why, with a few notable exceptions, there is little study and engagement with Hindu theology in theological schools, colleges, and universities. The advocates of Hindu theology are very few in number. In the study of the Hindu tradition, the religious studies approach, especially as exemplified in the historical and social scientific methods, prevails. These approaches have deepened and enriched our understanding of the history, character and workings of the Hindu tradition, but give less attention to the claim of the tradition to reveal important truths about the nature of reality that are essential for human well-being and to the evaluation and normative implications of such claims. In these essays, I do not shy away from speaking normatively about the Hindu tradition and its teachings. This will be evident in a special way in my three essays on liberation, but also in my essays on Hindu spirituality and on Hindu-Christian relationships.

The Hindu tradition, as I describe it in the first chapter of this work, is vast and diverse, and scholars must exercise caution about generalization. Although my essays in this volume draw from various Hindu traditions, these reflect, in a special way, the influence of the Hindu Advaita (nondual) tradition. This is the primary tradition of my scholarship and my commitment. Advaita refers to one of several Hindu traditions that are based in the recognition of the four Vedas (*Ṛg, Sāma, Yajur* and *Atharva*) as sources of authoritative teachings. More specifically, Advaita looks to the final or wisdom sections of the Vedas, the *Upaniṣads*, as the repository of the highest teachings. For this reason, the tradition is more accurately described as Advaita Vedānta (lit."end of the Veda") to acknowledge the specific authoritative significance of the *Upaniṣads*. Advaita acknowledges a line of distinguished teachers for the exegesis, clarification, defense and transmission of its teachings. There is no dispute, however, that the principal systematizer, exponent, and apologist for Advaita is Śaṅkara (ca.788–820). Śaṅkara's legacy to the tradition are his commentaries on the *Bhagavadgītā*, the Brahmasūtras, and on ten of the *Upaniṣads* (*Īśa, Kena, Kaṭha, Praśna, Māṇḍūkya* and *Kārikā, Muṇḍaka, Aitareya, Bṛhadāraṇyaka, Chāndogya* and *Taittirīya*). Śaṅkara interpreted the *Upaniṣads* to teach that the infinite *brahman* is the source of the universe. Its relationship with the universe is properly described as not-two (Advaita). *Brahman* is identical with the human self (*ātmā*) and constitutes the single ontological truth of everything that exists, even as clay is the truth of all clay objects. Knowledge of the identity obtaining between *brahman* and *ātmā* overcomes ignorance and constitutes liberation (*mokṣa*).[4]

My essays in this volume are organized broadly by themes into three sections: Theology, Dialogue and Liberation. I begin (chapter one) with a general introductory discussion on the Hindu tradition. This is a quick survey for the reader who may lack familiarity with the vocabulary, primary texts, doctrines, and social structures of the Hindu tradition. The primary context for this discussion is the Hindu tradition in the United States. I begin with a description of the ritual installation of the main *mūrti* (icon) at the Hindu temple in Maple Grove, Minnesota, and end with some reflections on the future of the tradition outside of India.

Chapter two expands on the nature of the sacred text as a valid source of knowledge (*pramāṇa*) and the implications of this argument. When a text is categorized as a valid source of knowledge, the arguments for its authority cannot be centered solely on its origin. In this case, the validity of the text is dependent on its ability to satisfy the twofold criteria of valid knowledge. It must inform us of a subject matter that cannot be ascertained through the operation of another means of knowledge, and its claims must not be contradicted by anything established through other valid sources. This approach places the scripture in the wider stream of discourse about the nature of reality and is opposed to the compartmentalization of human knowledge. A belief or proposition that is contradicted loses its validity. If a religious teaching contradicts a well-established fact of experience, it cannot be considered authoritative. In this chapter, I consider also how such view of the sacred text allows for a refutation of the structures of caste.

In chapter three, I employ a definition of spirituality as the way we ought to live our lives in relation to our understanding of the ultimate. Starting with the problem of greed and its roots in a false understanding of self, I regard the overcoming of greed as a primary fruit of Hindu spirituality. The focus of Hindu spirituality is life in this world, here and now. Hindu spirituality does not propose the rejection of the world, but a transformed way of being in the world; a way of being in the world that is characterized by freedom from greed. It draws us into a deep unity with all beings, affirms the dignity and worth of all, and promotes compassion and consideration for the common good.

The four essays in Section Two (Dialogue) focus, in a special, but not exclusive way, on Hindu Christian relationships. Chapter four begins by identifying the special regard Hindus like Ram Mohan Roy, Swami Vivekananda and Gandhi had for Jesus. Hindu interpreters have noted the similarities in the symbols and images, examples and parables, used by Jesus in speaking about the religious life. They commend his freedom from greed, his transparent nonpossessiveness and generous self-giving. At the same time, Christians are often frustrated by the scant regard some Hindus have for religious differences. It is necessary that we acknowledge our differences, learn in humility from each other, and deepen the friendship. It is important that Hindus and Christians come together in dialogue on divisive issues such as conversion and caste. We need relationships that enable us to listen and to share, to ask questions and to be questioned. We need relationships that inspire cooperative action to overcome unjust and oppressive structures of all kinds and that work to heal and transform our communities through the practice of justice.

In chapter five, I return to the significance of the *mūrti* in the Hindu temple and worship, and consider the implications of such worship for persons of other faiths. Some from the traditions of Judaism, Christianity and Islam equate *mūrti* with idol and condemn Hindu worship as being idolatrous. Although the choice to participate in the worship of a different tradition must be made on the basis of one's own theological commitments, it is important that understanding of other traditions be truthful. If we define idolatry as the false equation of the infinite divine with a finite object, this contravenes the Hindu self-understanding. Hindu theological traditions, both nondual and dual, emphasize the immanence and transcendence of the divine. Similarly, along with the multiple representations of the divine, there is a theological understanding of divine unity and oneness. This understanding of divine transcendence and oneness is not elitist, but widely shared by Hindus.

Having noted in chapter five the generally positive regard for Jesus among Hindu commentators, chapter six offers a detailed examination and evaluation of Swami Vivekananda's interpretation of the meaning of Jesus. Vivekananda emphasized Jesus' otherworldliness, and his commitment to the life of renunciation. Vivekananda had little or no interest in the historical Jesus. In his view, the Christian tradition erred in making the messenger the message. He spoke of Christ as a universal state of being and of Jesus as someone who had perfectly attained this state. Vivekananda does not rely upon Christian theological interpretations for his understanding of Jesus. Although this allows him to view Jesus through the categories of Hindu nondualism, ignoring a theological tradition runs the risk of offering interpretations that have no credibility within the tradition and that have no impact on the tradition's self-understanding. At the same time, he universalized the message of Jesus beyond the boundaries of Christianity, commended Jesus to his fellow Hindus, and suggested that there may be a distinctive nondual understanding of Jesus' relationship with God that may enrich Christian theological understanding,

Chapter seven explores the interreligious relationships through the lens of friendship. Employing a fourfold description of the characteristics of friendship drawn from the 15th century poet, Tulasidasa (shared identity, ethical responsibilities, trust, and generosity), I examine the relationship between Mahatma Gandhi (1869–1948) and his closest Christian friend, Charles Freer Andrews (1871–1940). Though differing in background and training, Gandhi and Andrews found common ground in their commitment to truth-seeking and service. They recognized that the truth they sought was greater than the traditions to which they belonged and they sought to learn from each other. They were united also in the conviction that the God they served lived in all beings and in creation, and that love for God must find expression in life as a servant. Although they disagreed, sometime publicly, on major issues, their trust created a safe space for mutual questioning and criticism. Criticism of their relationship from members of their respective traditions did not weaken their tie of friendship. They were generous in sharing and in receiving. The love, trust, sharing, and critical questioning that their relationship exemplified are vital for understanding meaningful interreligious relations in our times.

The three essays in Section Three (Liberation) build on my work on Hindu liberation theology.[5] In chapter eight, I identify what I regard as the major theological challenges to the development of Hindu liberation theology. These include: indifference to the world and the conditions of human life; interpretations of the meaning of liberation (*mokṣa*) that equate it entirely with freedom from the world and from the cycle of birth, death and rebirth; rigid interpretations of *karma* that dispose us to seeing all forms of suffering, and even injustice and oppression, as deserved; the hierarchies of caste; and the dominance of the ideology of Hindutva. Conversely, a Hindu theology of liberation requires a value for the world ontologically, and an understanding of the meaning of liberation (*mokṣa*) that values life in this world and that details the ethical implications of *mokṣa* for the transformation of human relationships and social structures. In addition, such a theology requires an affirmation of the equal worth and dignity of all human beings as well as an expanded understanding of suffering and a commitment to working for its overcoming. The work of developing this theology will not be meaningfully undertaken without attentive listening to the voices of those who experience the tradition as denying them the opportunity and resources to flourish.

Chapter nine examines the caste order of Hindu society in relation to the aspiration for the dignity and equality of all human beings. I focus on the *Bhagavadgītā* and on post-independence Indian Hindu commentaries on the thirteenth verse of chapter four ("The four *varṇas* were created by Me, differentiated by qualities (*guṇa*) and action (*karma*); although I am the creator, know Me to be the immutable nondoer.") I also highlight salient arguments against some of these interpretations by the Dalit leader, Dr. B. R. Ambedkar (1891–1956).

Hindu commentators, on the whole, do not problematize this text but treat the fourfold order as divinely ordained. There is no acknowledgement in these commentaries of the dehumanization, indignities, and injustices inflicted on the untouchables. Some commentators even suggest that one's place in the caste order does not or should not matter if one's aim is liberation and one performs one's work worshipfully. These interpretations and others discussed in this chapter are carefully and vigorously contested by Dr. Ambedkar. For example, none of these commentators interrogate the necessity for caste labels. Ambedkar, on the other hand, contends that as long as these names are retained, the hierarchies higher and lower will persist. It is regrettable that Hindu commentators do not engage the sharp criticisms of Dr. Ambedkar, with the consequence that they repeat interpretations that he refuted. Ambedkar believed that there were teachings in the Hindu tradition to challenge caste inequality, but Hindus failed to connect theology with life.

A theology of liberation must also aim for positive peace and human reconciliation. Chapter ten, the final chapter in this work, identifies and considers Hindu theological resources that contribute to these ends. One of the central insights of the Hinduism, consistently proclaimed by its diverse traditions, is the unity of all existence in God. The significance which Hinduism grants to the truth of life's unity may be appreciated from the fact that its discernment is considered to be the hallmark of wisdom and liberation. It is from the perspective of life's unity and our shared unity that we question unjust human relationships. It is the same perspective which urges us to overcome estrangement, and work for reconciliation.

The view that the human problem at its most fundamental level is one of ignorance and that this ignorance expresses itself in our failure to discern the unity of all existence is central to the development of a Hindu approach to reconciliation. It enables us to see the other, the one with whom we disagree and with whom we may be locked in struggle, as a fellow human being.

The traditions of Hinduism offer resources that justify and inspire the work of reconciliation. The challenge is to highlight these core teachings to simultaneously employ these teachings as the basis of a rigorous Hindu self-examination which identifies oppressive structures. It is easy to succumb to the temptation of speaking in platitudinous ways about the need and value for reconciliation while ignoring the challenges of addressing and overcoming these structures that sanction and enable some human beings to inflict suffering on other human beings. Reconciliation will always remain an intangible ideal as long as we are unwilling to unearth and confront the underlying causes of human conflict and divisiveness.

As I noted earlier, most of the scholarship about the Hindu tradition done in the western academy employs the methodologies of the social sciences and the history of religions. My voice in these essays is that of a committed and critical scholar of my tradition and I am not hesitant to speak normatively. Readers will also discover that I am not reluctant to speak critically about structures of injustice within my tradition and to do so on the basis of those Hindu values that affirm human dignity and value. I hope therefore, that these essays will be used in undergraduate, graduate and seminary courses, in which teachers and students find it beneficial to engage with the Hindu tradition theologically. I strive intentionally to write also for a larger reading community and I hope that interested Hindus and readers from other traditions will find these essays useful for deepening and challenging their understanding of the tradition.

References

1 Francis X. Clooney, *Comparative Theology* (West Sussex: Wiley-Blackwell, 2010), 9.

2 The nature of scripture as *pramāṇa* is the focus of my discussion in chapter two of this work. For a very detailed treatment of Śaṅkara's understanding of the Vedas as a *prāmaṇa* see my earlier work, *Accomplishing the Accomplished: The Vedas as a Source of Valid Knowledge in Śaṅkara* (Honolulu: University of Hawaii Press, 1991).

3 I have argued elsewhere that the championing of experience (*anubhava*) over scripture is one of the primary reasons for the decline of Hindu theology in contemporary times. See Anantanand Rambachan, *The Limits of Scripture: Vivekananda's Reinterpretation of the Vedas* (Honolulu: University of Hawaii Press, 1994).

4 For my exposition of the Advaita tradition, see Anantanand Rambachan, *The Advaita Worldview: God, World and Humanity* (Albany: State University of New York Press, 2006).

5 See Anantanand Rambachan, *A Hindu Theology of Liberation: Not-Two is Not One* (Albany: State University of New York Press, 2015).

PART I

THEOLOGY

CHAPTER ONE

HINDU TRADITIONS: UNITY AND DIVERSITY

A New Hindu Temple in Minnesota

During the weekend of June 29–July 2, 2006, the Hindu community in Minnesota celebrated the opening of its new temple, located in the city of Maple Grove. The central icon (*mūrti*) of the temple is God as Vishnu. He is represented in icon form as Śrī Varadarāja Swāmi (Lord of Blessings) and is accompanied by his feminine counterparts, Srī Lakshmi (Goddess of Wealth) and Śrī Bhūdevī (Goddess of the Earth). The Varadarāja icon of Vishnu is modeled after a temple and a *mūrti* (icon) by the same name, in the south Indian city of Kanchipuram. A traditional verse (*kṣetram gītam*) was composed, celebrating Vishnu's new abode in the city of Maple Grove:

> I bow in respect and offer worship to:
> Śrī Varadarāja Swāmi, who is Lord of Śrī Bhūdevī and Śrī Lakshmi;
> Who has the city of Maple Grove as His auspicious abode and liberates us from sins, as He is kind and compassionate;
> Who resides in the divine Minnesota Temple, bestows bliss in both worlds, and is realized by His devotees;
> Who is the refuge to many kinds of seekers and fosters tolerance and peace;
> Who shines with splendor along with deities such as Shiva, Durga, Ganesha, Skandha, and who is worshipped in a thousand names such as Rama, Krishna and Govinda.[1]

The significance of this composition, praising God as having a new sacred abode in the city of Maple Grove, has to be seen in the context of the widely shared Hindu teaching that, in a properly consecrated icon, God becomes accessible for worship. At the center of this consecration ritual are the procedures of *kumbhābhiṣekam* (anointing with sacred water) and *prāṇapratiṣṭha* (establishing the life force), both of which are believed to transform a granite sculpture into a living embodiment of

God. According to Rāmānuja (eleventh century), the foremost Vaiṣṇava theologian, the icon embodiment (*arcāvatāra*) is one of the five ways in which God manifests.[2] In his supreme form (*para*), God eternally abides in the heavenly world. The emanations (*vyūhas*) of God preside over the functions of creation, preservation, and destruction. At periodic intervals, God incarnates, and persons such as Rama and Krishna are believed to be earthly incarnations (*avatāras*) of God. God resides in the heart of all beings as the inner controller (*antaryāmin*). Finally, and most importantly for Vaiṣṇavas, is the presence of God in the icon (*arcāvatāra*). It is an act of grace that makes worshipful interaction (*pūja*), especially in the temple, possible and meaningful.

Planting Hindu Roots in the United States

The inauguration of the new Hindu temple in Maple Grove is a milestone in the evolution and effort of the growing Hindu community in Minnesota. A temple is one of the important ways by which Hindus express their identity with a new place, and their hope for the future of their tradition. It is a statement that the community now understands itself to be a permanent part of the religious landscape of the United States. The story of the Hindus in Minnesota is a replication of the experience of Hindu communities in cities across the United States.

Most of the elders of this community came to the United States during the latter half of the 1960s and early 1970s in search of higher education and professional training. They came with the intention of returning to India with their newly acquired skills since, prior to 1965, they were not eligible for American citizenship. In 1923, the United States Supreme Court had ruled that Hindus could not be citizens of the United States. "Hindu" was interpreted as a racial and not a religious category.[3] The case that resulted in this ruling involved an application for United States citizenship by Bhagat Singh Thind, a Sikh settled in Canada. The court argued that Hindus were not "free white persons" under the law and, therefore, not entitled to citizenship. A federal law of 1790 permitted only white immigrants to become naturalized citizens. The Immigration Act of 1924 established a national origins quota that excluded Indians, along with immigrants from China, Korea, and Japan, from entering the United States.

The year 1965 marked a turning point in the history of the Hindu community in the United States. The Immigration Act of 1965, initiated by President John F. Kennedy and signed into law by President Lyndon B. Johnson, at a ceremony at the foot of the Statue of Liberty, eliminated national origins quotas, and made it possible for significant numbers of

Asians and other non-Europeans to take the first steps to becoming citizens of the United States. This opportunity was embraced by most of the Hindus residing in Minnesota.

Although the Immigration Act of 1965 was restrictive in the sense that it gave priority to immigrants with professional skills, the influx of Indian immigrants to the United States was significant. The 1980 census listed 387,223 "Asian Indians" as permanent residents. In the 1990 census, this number had climbed to around 1.7 million. The estimated Hindu population in the United States is now over 2 million.[4] As a consequence of the restrictive immigration policy, they constitute a distinct group, "with a higher proportion of educated and skilled individuals than Indian populations elsewhere in the world."[5] They are concentrated largely in the metropolitan areas of New York, New Jersey, Illinois, Texas, and California, although there are few urban areas without a Hindu presence.

Minnesota Hindu families soon turned their attention from professional endeavors to the preservation and transmission of religious and cultural traditions. They were concerned about a new generation of American-born Hindus developing a Hindu identity and being enriched by the insights of the Hindu worldview. Lacking the resources to acquire or construct a building for the purpose of worship, families gathered at each other's homes to study the *Bhagavadgītā*, perform traditional rituals, and celebrate festivals. These informal family gatherings were the genesis of the formation, in 1978, of the Hindu Society of Minnesota, and the acquisition, in the same year, of a church building in northeast Minneapolis. After appropriate renovations and the construction of an altar to house the *mūrtis*, the building was formally opened for use on February 17, 1979, and became the center of Hindu religious activity for the next 27 years.

During this period, a pattern of worship developed that was quite different from that in a traditional Hindu temple. Every Sunday morning, between the hours of 10.30 a.m. and 12 p.m., devotees gathered for a congregational worship experience consisting of devotional songs (*bhajans*), chanting the names of God (*kīrtan),* and recitation of prayers and sacred verses (*mantras*).[6] Worship culminated at noon with the performance of the *ārati* ceremony and the distribution of *prasāda*.[7] At the heart of the Sunday worship (*satsangh*), however, was a discourse delivered by a lay leader, followed by a question and answer period. This gave the speaker an opportunity to develop and expand a particular theme and enabled the congregation to contribute insights drawn from their own study and life experiences.

This congregational form of worship at a fixed time, consisting of singing, chanting, rituals, discourse, and discussion, is different from the pattern of worship in India, where temple visits continue to be an individual, largely unstructured, experience. Temple architecture in the United States is already reflecting the need and emphasis on forms of Hindu worship that have a more communal and collective character; these now usually occur in large halls facing an altar, on which *mūrtis* of the major Hindu deities are located. It is clear that we will continue to see an emphasis on the more congregational forms of Hindu worship and the development of temple forms that will adapt to new community needs. The Hindu Society of Minnesota also exemplifies a pattern of lay participation in the administrative and liturgical life of the Hindu temple. Before the construction of the new temple in Maple Grove, it managed, for almost two decades, without the services of a trained ritual specialist (*pūjārī*) and visitors from India were always surprised to learn that they could approach the *mūrti* and make their own prayerful offerings.[8] Annual Hindu camps for boys and girls have become a regular feature of the temple's activity. These are run by laypeople and offer an intensive exposure to basic elements of Hindu practice and belief.

Worship in Temple and Home

The presence of a properly consecrated *mūrti* implies that the temple is the dwelling place of God. It is a sacred environment where everything is centered and focused on God. In temple and home worship, God is honored through a series of hospitality offerings made before the icon. These are generally about sixteen in number and include the initial invocation of the deity, the invitation to a seat, the washing of the feet, and acts of adoration through the offering of flowers, the burning of incense, the waving of lights, and the consecration of food. Worship always concludes with the offering of *prasāda*, that is, food which has been ritually offered to God. *Prasāda* means blessing or gift, and is a reminder, for Hindus, of the generosity of God. Visitors to a Hindu temple routinely bring fruits and other edibles, that are offered to God and returned as *prasāda* to be shared with family and friends.

For most Hindus, the primary purpose of visiting a temple, like the one in Maple Grove, Minnesota, is to have a *darśan* of the icon. The Sanskrit word, *darśan*, literally means "seeing," but it is used specifically to describe the visual apprehension of the sacred. Hindus stand with reverential gazes before the icon, experiencing a profound sense of being in God's all-encompassing presence. Most approach the *mūrti* with eyes open, but, as the sense of the divine fills their hearts and minds, their eyes spontaneously close in order to experience, more fully, the sacred moment. Seeing does not become *darśan* unless it awakens the awareness of God.

Darśan is a dual mode of experience. While it is a profound sense of seeing or being awake to God's reality, it is, at the same time, a deep consciousness of being "seen" by God or standing in God's presence. In *darśan*, Hindus see and know that they exist in divine awareness. To enhance this experience, the eyes of the icon are usually prominent and conspicuous. The final ceremony in the ritual installation of a *mūrti*, referred to as *prāṇapratiṣṭha*, involves the opening of the eyes. A *mūrti* with eyes closed does not engender, easily, the sense of being seen by God.

The elaborate worship rituals performed in the Hindu temple are replicated, in simpler forms, in Hindu homes. Most Hindu homes have a special room or corner set aside for the purpose of *pūja*. The family's favorite representations of God (*iṣṭadevātas*) and the utensils used in worship are kept there. This area of each home has an atmosphere of sanctity and is the focus of the family's religious life. Great care is taken to maintain its purity and cleanliness.

There is great variation in the forms of worship occurring in Hindu homes, depending on factors such as competence, family circumstance and personal preference. In some homes, for example, a complete *pūja* ritual is performed daily by a competent family member. In most homes, however, the full ritual will only be conducted a few times each year on special occasions. Daily worship generally takes the form of a few selected procedures from the *pūja* ritual, such as the offerings of light, incense or flowers. Portions of sacred texts, such as the *Bhagavadgītā* and Rāmāyaṇa, may be read, and the names of God recited. These are usually performed twice daily, in the mornings and evenings. The mother in the Hindu home, who plays a significant role in the transmission of the religious tradition, commonly takes the initiative and plays a leading role in family worship.

As in the case of the Hindu temple, the presence of a *mūrti* transforms the family home into an abode of God. The *mūrti* is a potent reminder of God's presence and the home becomes a sacred space, in which all aspects of life are centered on God. In the *mūrti*-form, God is the beloved household guest around whom all activities revolve and to whom everything is dedicated.

Traditionally, the Hindu home is the center of religious life and all of the sacraments (*saṁskāras*), marking important stages in the life of the individual, are performed in the home. Among the most important of such rites are those concerned with the birth of a child, one's initiation into religious life, marriage, and death. All of these are essentially religious in nature and are occasions for family gatherings and worship. In recent times, however, particularly in Hindu communities outside of India, there is the increasing tendency to perform such ceremonies in the temple and not in the home, and the architecture of the temples is already accommodating these changing needs.

Unity and Diversity

The rich traditions that are being preserved and transformed in the United States belong to one of the world's most ancient religions. It is astonishingly diverse, incorporating numerous streams of influence. "Hindu" is not the personal name of a founder or sage, whose teachings are followed by members of this religion. It does not identify or describe a central doctrine or practice. "Hindu" is the Iranian version for the name of a river that was referred to variously as the "Sindhu," "Indos," and "Indus." Those who lived on the land drained by the river were derivatively called "Hindus." They did not share a uniform religious culture and the Hindu tradition today continues to shelter a multiplicity of perspectives and practices.

Among these are the beliefs and practices of the numerous tribal communities across India, the extensive Indus valley civilization that covered a significant area of northern India, the distinctive traditions of southern India and the hymns, ritual practices and theology compiled in the body of texts known as the Vedas. To these and other influences, we must add the encounters with Christianity, Islam and western thought in the modern period. The consequence is an ancient, large and many-branched family, recognizable through vital common features, but preserving also the rich uniqueness of its individual members.

Organizationally, the tradition is highly decentralized. There is no one person who speaks authoritatively for all Hindus or a central institution governing their affairs. Although there are doctrines to which most Hindus subscribe, doctrinal and ritual uniformity have never been sought or demanded. There are no creedal statements to which all Hindus must subscribe and no process of excommunication. Hinduism or *Sanatana Dharma* (Eternal Law), as many followers prefer, is a dynamic movement and flow of the forces of unity and diversity. It reflects the astonishing variation in geography, language, and culture across the Indian sub-continent. If we are attentive to this fact of diversity, then any summary of key teachings, texts and practices will not be misleading.

Texts: *Śruti* and *Smṛti*

Many of the vital common features of the Hindu family can be traced to the insights compiled in the texts referred to as the Vedas. "No other living tradition," writes Klaus Klostermaier, "can claim scriptures as numerous or as ancient as Hinduism; none can boast an unbroken tradition preserved as faithfully as the Hindu tradition."[9] In practice, Hindus look to a vast array of sacred texts (some in Sanskrit, others in vernacular languages) of India for guidance.[10]

For the purpose of understanding the range and character of oral and written texts in Hinduism, it is useful to employ a traditional orthodox classification of sacred texts into two groups: *śruti* and *smṛti*. *Śruti* means "that which is heard," while *smṛti* means "that which is remembered." In this classification, the term *śruti* is reserved for those texts that are believed to be revealed, while *smṛti* is used for texts with identifiable human authors, regarded as secondary in authority to the *śruti.* While the distinction is helpful for surveying the scriptures of Hinduism, it is important to keep in mind that many *smṛti* texts are understood by particular traditions to be revealed and enjoy considerable authority and prestige within those communities. The four Vedas (*Ṛg, Sāma, Yajur* and *Atharva*), however, are widely acknowledged by Hindus to be *śruti* and acceptance of the authority of the Vedas is commonly regarded as necessary for Hindu orthodoxy, even though such acceptance may be merely formal and nominal.

Each Veda has four sections: the *Samhita, Brāhmaṇa, Āraṇyaka* and *Upaniṣads.* Modern scholars regard this order as a chronological one and consider the *Samhitā* section of the *Ṛg Veda*, dated 1200 BCE or earlier, to be the oldest, and the *Upaniṣads*, dated 500 BCE or earlier, to be the latest. The *Samhitā* portion of each Veda is a collection of hymns addressed to different deities (*devatā*). The *Samhitā* of the *Ṛg Veda*, for example, is a collection of 1028 hymns consisting of over 10,000 verses. These hymns address and praise *devatās* associated with various phenomena. These include Agni (fire), Indra (heavens), Yama (death), and Varuna (waters). In recent times, Hindu scholars and practitioners have been concerned to explain that the plurality of deities in the *Samhitā* section of the Vedas does not imply polytheism. The Sanskrit, *deva*, or *devatā,* is commonly translated as God, even though the term *deva* means luminous and refers broadly to a divine entity.[11] *Devatās* are many, but the Ultimate is one.[12]

The *Brāhmaṇas* are prose texts that describe the rules for the performance of Vedic rituals. They provide an interpretation of the earlier texts, commenting on the meaning of the hymns, the rituals, the methods in which particular hymns are to be used, and the results to be achieved.

The *Āraṇyakas* (forest books) continue the interpretative process already discernible in the *Brāhmaṇas*, by providing symbolic and philosophical reflections on the rituals. Their concern is to direct attention from the outward ritual to their inner meaning and significance.

The trend toward philosophical reflection in the *Āraṇyakas* culminates in the *Upaniṣads*, the final section of each of the four Vedas. The word *Upaniṣad* is derived from the Sanskrit root "*sad*" which means "to destroy." *Upa* (near) and *ni* (ascertained knowledge) are prefixes. The word suggests a knowledge that destroys ignorance (*avidyā*) and leads to liberation (*mokṣa*). The *Upaniṣads* are in the form of dialogues between religious teachers and students on the nature of the self (*ātmā*), the absolute (*brahman*), and the world (*jagat*). Self-knowledge and not ritual action is presented in the *Upaniṣads* as the means to liberation.

Although the Vedas continue to enjoy special canonical status in Hinduism, it is true that the majority of Hindus encounter the material of the Vedas indirectly through the *smṛti* texts. Traditional study of the Vedas was limited to the male members of the first three castes (*brāhmaṇas, kṣatriyas* and *vaiśyas*). *Śūdras* and women were excluded from the study and hearing of the Vedas and were exposed only to *smṛti* literature. *Smṛti* texts generally legitimized their status by linking themselves to the authority of the Vedas, and all of them seek, in one way or another, to claim the sanction of the Vedas for their particular teachings. The large number of texts that are classified as *smṛti* precludes detailed discussion or even enumeration. I will focus on some that continue to be significant at the popular level.

The *Mahābhārata* (400 BCE–400 CE) is traditionally attributed to Vyāsa, although the name itself simply means "compiler." It is considered to be the longest work in Indian literary history and consists of over 100,000 verses. The main story of the *Mahābhārata* is clear, even though the text also narrates myths and events not connected with the central narrative. This narrative recounts the struggle between two set of cousins, the Pāṇḍavas and Kauravas, for a kingdom in north India. The Kaurava leader, Duryodhana, is power hungry and reluctant to do justice to his cousins. After futile efforts for a peaceful resolution, the parties engage in a climactic battle in which most of the warriors on both sides are killed, but from which the Pandavas emerge victorious.

One of the enduring legacies of the *Mahābhārata* is the *Bhagavadgītā* (Song of God). The *Bhagavadgītā* (150 BCE–250 CE), now widely abbreviated as the *Gītā*, is a dialogue of 700 verses, arranged in eighteen chapters, between Krishna and his Pandava friend and warrior, Arjuna. It constitutes chapters 23–40 of the *Bhīṣmaparvan* (Book 6) of the *Mahābhārata*. On the day of the great battle, Krishna, who had volunteered to serve as Arjuna's charioteer, is instructed by Arjuna to drive his chariot between the two armies so that he could survey the opposing forces. The prospect of having to fight against his relatives and teachers saps all enthusiasm from Arjuna and throws him into a moral crisis. Krishna used this moment to instruct Arjuna about the immortality of the self and the necessity of fulfilling his social duty as a warrior. Performing actions without selfish and egocentric motives is conducive to the attainment of liberation. The authority of the *Bhagavadgītā* is connected to the fact that Arjuna eventually discovers (chapter 11) that his advisor is none other than God, in one of his human incarnations. Even though formally a *smṛti*, the text is revered as the word of God and treated by its earliest commentators as revelation.

The *Rāmāyaṇa* (400 BCE–300 CE) is about a quarter of the length of the *Mahābhārata*; it is traditionally attributed to the poet Valmiki. It consists of seven books, narrating the life story of Rama, an incarnation of Vishnu and a prince of the north Indian kingdom of Ayodhya. Rama, heir to the throne of Ayodhya, is banished into exile at the request of his stepmother, Kaikeyi, who wishes for her own son, Bharata, to be the king. Rama calmly accepts his banishment because a promise of his father, Dasaratha, to his stepmother was at stake. His wife, Sita, and his brother, Lakshmana, accompany him. During their wandering as ascetics, Sita is kidnapped by Ravana, king of Sri Lanka, and taken to his island home. Rama assembles an army, rescues Sita, and returns to rule Ayodhya. Rama and Sita are venerated as models of virtue and the *Rāmāyaṇa* has been described as the Hindu's favorite book, exemplifying filial obedience, brotherly love and loyalty in marriage. There are vernacular versions in all the major languages of India.

Purāṇas (old, ancient) is the general term used for a group of eighteen Sanskrit texts compiled between 400 CE and 1000 CE. As a genre of religious literature, the *Purāṇas* are supposed to deal with five subjects: the origin of creation; the dissolution of the universe and its re-creation; genealogies of sages, kings, and deities; cosmic cycles ruled by the Manus; and the history of the solar and lunar dynasties. Each *Purāṇa* is centered on one or another of the major deities of Hinduism—Vishnu, Shiva, or Shakti. Devotees of a particular deity tend to selectively emphasize and give importance to the *Purāṇa* extolling that deity.

Like the *Purāṇas*, the *Āgamas* (ca.7–11 CE) center on the principal Hindu deities and are considered by their respective communities to be revealed. The Vaiṣṇava *Āgamas* center on the worship of God as Vishnu, the Saiva *Āgamas* on Shiva, and the Shakta *Āgamas*, also called *Tantras*, on the worship of the Goddess (*Shakti*). The *Tantras* present an elaborate and graded path to liberation, consisting of ritual worship, chanting, *mantra* recitation, and meditation. These practices must be undertaken under the guidance of a teacher and only after proper initiation.

In all of the regional languages of India, there are devotional works that are extremely popular. Their availability in the local dialects enhance their appeal. In South India, the *Divyaprabandham*, a collection of the songs of Śrīvaiṣṇava poets known as the *ālvārs* (500–850 CE), the *Tevāram* and the *Tiruvācakam* are among the most important devotional works in Tamil. Songs from these collections are widely used in daily temple and home worship. In north India, poetic compositions in Hindi and its various dialects live in the memories and daily recitations of millions. Among the well-known devotional poets of north India are Surdas (16th century), Kabirdas (15th century), and Mirabai (16th century). The verses of Tukaram (17th century) in Marathi and the Gujarati songs of Narsi Mehta (16th century) are recited daily. A relatively recent composition, the *Gitanjali* of Rabindranath Tagore (1861–1941), India's Nobel laureate, has already taken its place among India's devotional works. In its original Bengali and English translations, it is used in liturgical settings.

Teachings: The Four Goals of Hindu Life

Contrary to popular impression, Hinduism is neither life denying nor otherworldly. The goals that humans are capable of pursuing and achieving have been classified under four headings. Together, these are seen as essential to the realizing of the full potential of the human person. While it is necessary to discuss these goals in some order or sequence, one should not expect that their fulfillment also proceeds in a similar sequence. The ideal is a simultaneous pursuit and realization of all four ends and the achievement of balance among them.

Artha

The first component of the full human life is referred to, in Sanskrit, as *artha*. The term *artha* is very broad in its meaning and, while generally equated with wealth, includes also power, success, and social prestige. By acknowledging *artha* as a goal of life, Hinduism recognizes the need of every human being for access to those material necessities that make life possible and comfortable, and that enable one to fulfill social obligations.

While historically approving the voluntary renunciation of wealth in order to seek liberation, Hinduism has never given its blessings to involuntary poverty and material deprivation. The spirituality of Hinduism is not anti-materialistic.

Kāma

The second component of the good life is *kāma* (pleasure). *Kāma* includes sensual as well as aesthetic enjoyment. Sculpture, music, and dance flourished with the blessings of the Hindu tradition and Hindus love to celebrate life through these forms. *Kāma* legitimizes the human need and capacity for pleasure; the necessities of life are to be enjoyed as a way of fulfilling human nature. The goal of *kāma* reminds us that Hinduism is not life-negating or otherworldly. Hindus are not so spiritually minded that they despise the gain and enjoyment of material things.

While freely giving its approval to the pursuit of *artha* and *kāma*, the Hindu scriptures continually call our attention to the limitations of these twin ends. We are told that these, although legitimate, will never fully satisfy our deepest human needs and that their attainment will leave us incomplete. The reasons afforded are many. The gains of worldly pleasure and success are transient, leaving us hopelessly addicted to their momentary gratification. This is the insight of the *Bhagavadgītā* (5:22).

> Pleasures born of contact (between the body, senses, mind, and objects) are sources of pain, since they have a beginning and an end. The wise person is not content with these.[13]

Ultimately, in death, we leave wealth and worldly success behind.

There are other reasons, however, why *kāma* and *artha* leave us unsatisfied. Wealth, fame, and power are exclusive and, therefore, competitive and risky. The value and worth of these assets diminish when shared. One lives in uncertainty as to whether one's rivals will gain advantage, and hence one suffers from inadequacy and uncertainty. "The idea of a nation," writes Huston Smith, "in which everyone is famous is a contradiction in terms; if power were distributed equally no one would be powerful in the sense in which we customarily use the word. Fame consists in standing out from one's fellows and power is control over them. From the competitiveness of these values to their riskiness is one short step."[14]

The pursuit of *artha* and *kāma* does not distinguish us as a unique species of living beings. Other forms of life, in different degrees, have material needs and reflect a capacity for pleasure. It is the third component, *dharma*, that, in the first instance, distinguishes us as human beings.

Dharma

Dharma is a rich and multifaceted concept and, therefore, difficult to translate. The word is derived from the Sanskrit root meaning "to support or sustain" and can be partly equated with duty and virtue. *Dharma* emphasizes the social context in which we seek wealth and pleasure. Through *dharma*, we are reminded that the selfish and uncontrolled pursuit of wealth and pleasure lead to social chaos and disharmony. *Dharma* asks that we broaden our perspective to incorporate the good and well-being of the community. It reminds us that our rights are only possible and meaningful in a context where equal, if not greater, recognition is given to our duties and obligations. The personal attainment of wealth and pleasure, by inflicting pain and suffering on others, or by denying them the opportunity to freely seek these two ends, is opposed to *dharma*. In Hindu mythology, the symbol of *dharma* is the bull, whose four feet are truth, purity, compassion and generosity.

Karma and *Saṁsāra*

As a goal that presupposes freedom and choice, responsiveness to the requirements of *dharma* is highly valued within the Hindu tradition. Freedom and moral responsibility are also the basis for the Hindu faith in the interrelated doctrines of *karma* and *saṁsāra*. Briefly, Hindus understand the law of *karma* to mean that all actions performed, good or bad, will produce appropriate results, at some stage, in our lives. Through the law of *karma*, Hindus see the world as a moral stage and see us as living within the operation of a moral law. In the Hindu understanding, however, the moral consequences of our actions may not always be apparent during the course of the same life in which the actions are performed. Life is a pilgrimage, a journey of experience and learning through many different births towards liberation (*mokṣa*). Birth implies the association of the human self with a new physical body, while death implies the dissociation from that body. The law of *karma* or moral causation governs the journey through a continuous and connected series of life experiences, referred to as *saṁsāra*.

The doctrine of *karma* is often misunderstood as one that denies freedom of will and choice. It is argued that we lose all initiative and responsibility for actions if our experiences in the present life are determined by our actions in the past. Hindus sometimes cite the doctrine of *karma* to justify an attitude of fatalistic resignation and indifference to the circumstances of their lives. Properly understood, however, the law of *karma* emphasizes free will and insists upon moral responsibility. If, in my present life, I am experiencing the results and consequences of my past actions, this is only because I was responsible for these actions. The important point, of course, is that if I have influenced my present condition through my past behavior, there is no reason why I should not be able to shape my future through my present conduct. The law of *karma* stipulates that certain kinds of actions will naturally produce certain, consequences but this does not thereby paralyze our wills. On the contrary, it places responsibility squarely on our shoulders since it does not propose a power outside of ourselves that is responsible for our individual and collective destinies.

It is often argued also that belief in *karma* discourages efforts to relieve the suffering of others since misery is viewed as the just reward of undesirable actions in the past. It must be remembered, however, that the tradition that proposes *karma*, also asks us to respond continuously with compassion and generosity. If our fellow beings suffer because of improper choices in the past, it is also wrong of us, in the present, not to try, as best as we can, to comfort and aid them in their suffering. To justify our indifference by appealing to the doctrine of *karma* is a sad and pitiable way of shirking our duty to others. In the face of suffering, our responsibility is to work for its overcoming by addressing the causes, whether these are personal or structural.

Although emphasizing free will and responsibility, those interpretations of the doctrine of *karma* that comprehensively seek to explain all events in the present life as having causes that may be traced to actions performed earlier in this life or previous lives, are problematic. Such rigid interpretations of *karma* dispose us to seeing all forms of suffering, and even injustice and oppression, as explainable by actions in the past. In these interpretations, there is no injustice. The victim is responsible for their suffering and not the particular social or economic system that prevails. The perception of suffering as justified, undermines motivation to struggle for change. These interpretations of *karma* have also been deployed to argue for the hierarchical social order of caste; in this worldview, one is born into a caste and into all the socio-economic and cultural factors obtaining from this. Freedom from any caste is possible only by rebirth. These interpretations need to be vigorously contested.

Mokṣa

While the Hindu tradition ascribes great value to the practice of *dharma*, it does not see this as the ultimate goal of human existence. Hinduism's highest and most valued goal is *mokṣa*. The Sanskrit term *mokṣa* means freedom, and if we keep in mind the diversity of Hinduism, it is not inaccurate to say that this freedom is primarily from ignorance (*avidyā*). It is a common view in the Hindu tradition that ignorance of the true nature of the human self (*ātmā*) and the absolute (*brahman*) is the fundamental human problem and the underlying cause of suffering. Freedom or liberation cannot be obtained without right knowledge of reality.

According to three of the greatest theologians and traditions of Hinduism—Śaṅkara (ca. 8 CE) (Nondualism–Advaita), Rāmānuja (ca.12 CE) (Qualified Nondualism–Viśiṣṭādvaita), and Madhva (ca. 13 CE) (Dualism–Dvaita)—the self (*ātmā*) cannot be equated fully with the time-bound physical body or the ever-changing mind. In its essential nature, the self is eternal and infinite awareness. For Śaṅkara, the self is identical with *brahman;* for Rāmānuja, it is inseparably related to *brahman* as part to whole; and for Madhva, it is entirely different from but completely dependent on *brahman*.

Ignorant of the true nature of the self, one wrongly identifies it fully with the body and mind, imposes the limitations of these on the self, and becomes subject to insatiable greed and want. To obtain the objects of greed, one puts forth actions (*karma*) of various kinds. Greed-prompted actions generate results for which the performer of actions is responsible and which lead to subsequent rebirths in order to experience the consequences of these actions. All traditions of Hinduism adhere firmly to a belief in the doctrine of *karma* as a law of cause and effect that includes the moral dimensions of human life.

Mokṣa is consequent upon the right understanding of the nature of the self. While, as noted above, the nature of self is understood variously within the tradition, in all cases *mokṣa* implies the recognition of the self to be more than the psychophysical form, and to be immortal and full. Such an understanding of the self's essential nature, brings an end to the cycle of death, birth and rebirth. For Śaṅkara, liberation is possible while the individual is alive in the body. When one knows the self, one ceases to completely equate the self with the body, and one attains freedom. Liberation is not an end that must await the death of the body since the human problem is not synonymous with the fact of being alive but with ignorance (*avidyā* of *brahman*). It is not the absence of a body that constitutes liberation, but the overcoming of ignorance about God. The state of living liberation is referred to as *jīvanmukti* and the person is called a *jīvanmukta*. For Rāmānuja, on the other hand, the self can never recover its innate nature as long as it remains associated with the body. Freedom must await the death of the body. For all traditions of Hinduism, *mokṣa* implies freedom from suffering, greed and mortality.

Although the Hindu scriptures are hesitant to characterize the actual state of *mokṣa*, which defies all definition, the texts are not as reticent about the liberated person. Positively, liberation is the attainment of joy, since joy constitutes the very nature of *brahman*. When the student Bhṛgu, in the *Taittirīya Upaniṣad* (3.6.1) finally understood *brahman*, he understood it as the joy from which all things are born, by which they are sustained, and into which they return. *Brahman*, states *Bṛhadāraṇyaka Upaniṣad* (4.3.32), is supreme joy - "On a particle of this very joy other creatures live." In the *Chāndogya Upaniṣad* (7.1.13), Nārada goes to his teacher, Sanatkumāra, for knowledge of the self that frees from sorrow, and learns that the infinite alone is joy; there is no bliss in the finite.[15] Liberation is also equated, especially in the *Bhagavadgītā*, with the attainment of peace (*śanti*) and freedom from greed and possessiveness. It is the person who overcomes greed, and not the one who is a victim of greed, who obtains peace (2:70-71).

Liberation awakens us to a deeper identity and affinity with all beings. This is the outcome of understanding *brahman* to be the single source and ground of human selfhood. *Īśa Upaniṣad* (6-7)understands freedom from hate, sorrow and delusion to be a consequence of the knowledge of *brahman* existing in all beings.

> One who sees all beings in the self alone and the self in all beings, feels no hate by virtue of that understanding.
> For the seer of oneness, who knows all beings to be the self, where is delusion and sorrow?[16]

Liberation, in other words, does not alienate, isolate or separate one from the world and the community of beings, but awakens one to life's unity in God. In the *Bhagavadgītā,* the discussion on the identity of God in all, is followed by a text (6:32) praising the liberated as one who owns the joy and suffering of the other as one's own. On two occasions (5:25; 12:4), the text employs the expression, "delighting in the well-being of all" to describe the attitude of the liberated in relation to others. Liberation is equated with an empathetic way of being and living.

Social Structure: Caste and Untouchability

The *Ṛg Veda* has long been associated with the Aryans, a nomadic group commonly believed to have arrived in northern India, from north–central Europe, in around 1500 BCE, as invaders who conquered and dominated the native peoples. In recent times, however, a credible critique of the Aryan invasion hypothesis has been advanced,[17]

What is uncontested and important for our purposes is that the group that identified with the *Ṛg Veda* thought and referred to themselves as *ārya*s (noble, of noble descent, pure), defined themselves over and against others referred to as *dāsas* or *dāsyus*. The *dāsyus* were considered as subhuman, hypocritical, without virtue, observing different customs, and likened to a famine.[18]

By around 800 BCE, the *Ṛg Veda āryas* had consolidated themselves in relation to various non-*ārya* groups and systematized their relationship in the form of the hierarchically structured *varṇa* system. The *brāhmaṇas* (priests) occupied the top, followed by the *kṣatriyas* (soldiers), *vaishyās* (merchants and farmers) and *śūdras* (laborers). The first three groups are regarded as the *dvijas* or twice-born and are entitled to perform and participate in Vedic rituals. Most importantly, male members of these groups alone, underwent the initiatory ritual (*upanayana*) that enabled them to study the Vedas. The incorporation of the *śūdras* into the system, along with their servile status, supports the hypothesis that they represent the "others" who were gradually included into the complex social order. It is also possible that a policy of appeasement was practised, that rewarded cooperative non-*āryas* with elevation to membership in the upper *varṇas*.[19]

Not all non-*ārya* groups, however, were assimilated and incorporated. It is likely that some groups resisted or were not offered the "privilege" of becoming part of the *ārya* hierarchy. Such "hostile" groups, such as the *cāṇḍālas* and *śvapacas*, were declared ritually impure and segregated. The *cāṇḍālas*, for example, were equated with animals and considered unfit even to eat the remnants of another's meals. By the time of Manu (ca.150 BCE), it was believed that birth into a particular caste was the consequence of *karma* or the maturation of past moral actions in the present life. For bad deeds in this life, one could be reborn as a dog, a boar, or a *cāṇḍāla*, in this order. From its early use to refer to a specific group, *cāṇḍāla* became a general term for the untouchable other.

Numerous injunctions, based on general features of the *varna* system, such as the polarity of purity and impurity, hereditary occupations and the idea of the *dvija* (twice-born) led to the institution of innumerable injunctions against those groups now branded as *aspṛśya* (lit. untouchable). By the period between 400 BCE–400 CE, standard features of untouchability such as physical segregation, non-commensality and non-connubiality are firmly in place. The Vedas are not to be studied in a village where *cāṇḍālas* reside. Food offered in ritual is defiled if seen by a *cāṇḍāla* and sacrificial vessels are rendered impure by their touch. The texts specifying prohibitions against the *cāṇḍālas* group them with animals. Food and ritual vessels are polluted if seen and touched by dogs, crows and donkeys.

Omprakash Valmiki, in his autobiographical account *Joothan*, comments on the fact that "while it was considered all right to touch dogs and cats or cows and buffaloes, if one [a higher-caste person] happened to touch a Chuhra, one got contaminated and polluted." "The Chuhras," as Valmiki notes, "were not seen as human. They were simply things for use. Their utility lasted until the work was done. Use them and throw them away."[20] An upper caste person coming into contact with a *cāṇḍāla* was required to take a purificatory bath. *Cāṇḍālas* were to have separate wells, enter villages at night or during the day only if they identified themselves by a sound or with appropriate marks. For food, they must depend on others. A person stealing the animal of a *cāṇḍāla* was required to pay only half of the required fines. As Wilhelm Halbfass has rightly noted, the *cāṇḍālas* are part of the *dharmic* system through their exclusion from sacred ritual. "They participate in it so far as they accept their exclusion; they subject (or ought to subject) themselves to the ritual norms of exclusion and prohibition, and they are recognized as negative constituents of the system."[21]

Based on the recent Indian census (2011), members of the Scheduled Castes and Scheduled Tribes constitute twenty-five percent of India's population.[22] The Scheduled castes alone number over 200 million. Article 15 (1) of the Indian constitution specifies that "the State shall not discriminate against any citizen on grounds of religion, race, caste, sex, place of birth." Special laws, such as the Protection of Civil Rights Act, 1976, have been enacted to give meaning to constitutional provisions. In spite of such measures, however, the phenomenon of untouchability persists in contemporary India and Hindus continue to define the meaning of Hindu identity over and against those who are deemed polluting and, for this reason, marginalized. The distinctions between self and other, the boundaries of the pure and impure, are still drawn sharply in Indian villages, where the character of human and economic relationships is still governed by the hierarchies of caste, and where reports of violence against persons of lower castes are common.

Although the conditions of life in Indian cities are quite different from those obtaining in rural areas, cities are not free from the travails of caste and untouchability. In urban areas, discrimination expresses itself in more subtle forms, and in limited job choices that push untouchables to performing menial tasks. In a city like Hardwar, on the banks of the Ganges, physical segregation is evident in the fact that the upper caste dwellings are closer to the pure water of the river, while the lower castes are relegated, depending on relative degree of purity, to locations further away from the river.[23] Kancha Ilaiah has commented that the movement from rural to urban locations does not change the socioeconomic relations because of the pervasive character of caste. "We had hoped," writes Ilaiah, "that the decolonized Indian capital would make caste dysfunctional by giving us equal rights in politics, in economic institutions, cultural institutions, educational institutions and administrative institutions. But that has not happened. The migration from rural to urban centers has not changed our socioeconomic relations as caste discrimination has been built into every structure."[24]

We must acknowledge that, though occurring at a slow pace, changes are underway. The impact of legislation, urban life, democracy, freedom, equality and feminism are transforming age-old attitudes and customs. In addition, the modern era is also witness to increasing self-awareness among the untouchables and their readiness to organize themselves to agitate for justice. They are prepared also to embrace alternative religious options. The conversion of untouchables to traditions such as Buddhism, Christianity and Islam has evoked concern among several Hindu groups and some have responded with *śuddhi* (purifying) rituals, to admit them back into the fold of Hinduism. They are thought of as apostates who must be saved from the clutches of others and brought back to their original faith.

It is important that the role of religion and religious doctrine in providing legitimacy for the system of caste must be examined. This is a point well understood by the Dalit leader, Dr. Bhimrao Ambedkar (1891-1956).[25] A self-critical sincerity is needed to acknowledge the ways in which many, especially those from the so-called untouchable castes, experience the tradition as oppressive and as negating their dignity and self-worth. The fact that the religion into which one is born may not be liberative, must be admitted. There must be the will for the reform and reconstruction of Hindu society on the basis of those central insights and values of Hinduism that promote justice, dignity and the equal worth of human beings. The doctrine of divine equality, so deeply established at the heart of Hinduism, must become a powerful searchlight, illumining and healing exploitative and oppressive structures of Hindu society.

The Future: Challenges and Opportunities

While the traditions of Hinduism were transported outside the borders of India since ancient times, particularly to places in South and South-East Asia, the contemporary establishment of Hinduism outside of India is without historical precedent. The future of Hinduism in the United States will depend upon and will be shaped by the ways in which it deals with the exigencies of its circumstances, that are historically unique.

Historically, Hinduism has embraced both religion and culture, and the disentanglement of one from the other is quite difficult. It is significant that there is no Sanskrit equivalent for the word "religion," and the term *dharma*, sometimes equated with religion, is far more inclusive. The detachment of religion and culture, however, is rapidly becoming a reality in the experience of a new generation of Hindus born in the western world. The unity of religion and culture is being severed and the traditionally pervasive influence of Hinduism is relegated to fewer areas of life. How will the Hindu tradition develop and thrive in a context in which it does not exert a pervasive cultural influence? What forms will it assume and what would it mean to be a Hindu?

The unity of religion and culture obviated the need for special agencies for the transmission of the tradition. It was correctly assumed that a child would receive the necessary religious exposure by the mere fact of growing up in a particular community. The conditions of life in modern western societies, however, invalidate such an assumption. In a secular society of competing cultural and religious choices, the future of Hinduism can no longer be guaranteed by the fact of birth. The fact of birth will not be a sufficient reason for being a Hindu and, for the first time, increasing numbers of Hindus will be Hindus by choice and will have to be reconverted or converted to Hinduism. They will choose Hinduism from a variety of options available. Hinduism in the next millennium will be challenged to define itself with precision in relation to a variety of competing choices. Appeals on the basis of antiquity and the authority of tradition may not be very persuasive. Its challenges today are quite different from the Buddhist and Jain refutation of Vedic authority and a personal deity and its responses will have to be appropriate.

Successful strategies and agencies will have to be developed to ensure transmission from one generation to another. The evolution of such methods may prove quite challenging, for a number of reasons, to the Hindu tradition. While doctrinal issues have been debated vigorously by Hindu philosophers and teachers throughout the ages, it is accurate to say that in the transmission of the tradition, the emphasis has been on orthopraxis. In the western world, influenced heavily by the Christian stress on orthodoxy, Hindus are increasingly challenged to articulate and transmit their tradition in a manner that places more emphasis on its doctrinal content and stance. Hinduism will be challenged into a more explicit and self-conscious reflection and articulation of its world-view. There is a rich tradition of intellectual debate and discussion in Hinduism and a concern for doctrinal clarity and definition. The recovery of this often-neglected tradition will serve Hinduism well in its advent into the future.

While the problems are complex and challenging, there are promising signs of innovation and resilience in the diaspora. Many new temples in the west still have a regional character and following, but there are increasing numbers of new temples which serve the needs of Hindus of diverse regional and linguistic backgrounds and which bring together Hindus from the Indian sub-continent and those from parts of the Caribbean and Africa. They share a common rootedness in the traditions of Hinduism and this may eventually override the particularities of language and geography, as these recede in the memory of a new generation. Temple architecture is already reflecting the need and emphasis on those forms of Hindu worship that have a more communal and collective character and worship services now usually occur in large halls facing an altar on which *mūrtis* of the major Hindu deities are located. Most temples have regularly scheduled worship services, many on Sunday mornings, in which a communal worship service consisting of congregational singing, ritual and a lecture are essential ingredients. It is clear that we will continue to see an emphasis on the more congregational forms of Hindu worship and the development of temple forms which will adapt to new community needs. As it has done many times before, one of the world's oldest religious traditions is already responding creatively and resourcefully to its new challenges.

References

1 Composed by Sriram Pidaparti and published in a souvenir (2006) to commemorate the inauguration of the temple.

2 A Vaiṣṇava is one who worships God as Vishnu.

3 See Diana Eck, *Encountering God: A Spiritual Journey from Bozeman to Banaras* (Boston: Beacon Press, 1993), 34-36.

4 "Hindu Demographics," https://www.hafsite.org/hinduism-101/hindu-demographics.

5 Gurinder Singh Mann, Paul David Numrich and Raymond B. Williams, *Buddhists, Hindus, and Sikhs in America* (New York: Oxford University Press, 2001), 67.

6 A *bhajan* is a song of devotion. Many date back to the medieval period, that witnessed a great flowering of the devotional movement. Songs by saintly composers of that time, like Kabir, Surdas, Tulasidasa and the female poet, Mirabai, are sung daily in homes and temples. Most of the themes of these songs center around the incarnations of Rama and Krishna. They describe the attributes of God and the compassionate nature of God's activities. A *kīrtan*, on the other hand, is a musical recitation of the various names of God. Each name defines an attribute of God and several such names are combined and sung repeatedly.

7 *Ārati* is the waving of a flame before the *mūrti* in a clockwise direction. The flame is then carried to the members of the congregation, who pass their hands over the flame and touch their eyes and forehead. *Ārati* is a ceremony of adoration and reverence and light is one of the central symbols for God.

8 In 2000, a *pūjari* was employed on a full-time basis. His participation in the Sunday worship continued to be minimal and lectures were still delivered by laypersons. After the construction of the new temple in Maple Grove, several traditionally trained priests were appointed.

9 Klaus Klostermaier, *A Survey of Hinduism* (Albany: State University of New York Press, 1994), 65.

10 For a detailed discussion, see Anantanand Rambachan, "Hinduism," in *Experiencing Scripture in World Religions*, ed. Harold Coward (Maryknoll: Orbis Books, 2000), 85-112.

11 Klostermaier, *A Survey of Hinduism*, 130-154. He uses the term "polydevataism" instead of "polytheism."

12 Swami Prabhavananda, *The Spiritual Heritage of India* (California: Vedanta Press, 1979), 34-35. He cites the *Ṛg Veda* text, *ekam sat vipra bahudha vadanti* (being is one; sages speak in many ways), to explain that deities are many expressions of one God.

13 *The Bhagavadgītā*, trans. Winthrop Sargeant (Albany: State University of New York Press, 1993).

14 See Huston Smith, *The Religions of Man* (New York: Harper, 1965),19-20.

15 *Upaniṣads,* trans. Patrick Olivelle (New York: Oxford University Press, 1996).

16 My translation.

17 See Klaus Klostermaier, *A Survey of Hinduism*, 33-39.

18 See Prabhati Mukherjee, *Beyond the Four Varnas : The Untouchables in India* (Shimla: Indian Institute of Advanced Study, 1988),18-19.

19 See Mukherjee, *Beyond the Four Varnas*, 41-69.

20 Omprakash Valmiki, *Joothan*, trans. Arun Prabha Mukherjee (New York: Columbia University Press, 2003), 2. For another account of the experience of growing up as an untouchable in India, see Narendra Jadhav, *Untouchables* (New York: Scribner, 2005).

21 Wilhelm Halbfass, *India and Europe: An Essay in Understanding* (Albany: State University of New York Press), 126-127.

22 "SCs, STs form 25% of population, says Census 2011 data," http://archive.indianexpress.com/news/scs-sts-form-25--of-population-says-census-2011-data/1109988/.

23 See Julius Lipner, *Hindus: Their Religious Beliefs and Practices* (London: Routledge, 1994), 116-117.

24 Kancha Ilaiah, *Why I Am Not A Hindu* (Delhi: Samya, 1996), 68.

25 See, B. R. Ambedkar, *Annihilation of Caste*, ed. and annotated S. Anand, with introduction by Arundhati Roy (London: Verso Books, 2014).

CHAPTER TWO

PRĀMAṆA: UNDERSTANDING THE AUTHORITY OF SCRIPTURE

In Chapter 1, I used words like "scripture" and "sacred texts" to describe the Vedas and other sources of Hindu teaching. These terms are not meant to suggest homogeneity across traditions in understanding the significance of these sources. Such homogenization leads to an unfortunate loss of the distinctive understandings of religious traditions and the enrichment that such differences make possible.

Although the Vedas share similarities with the sacred sources of other traditions, the classical Vedānta traditions have developed and articulated a distinct argument for their nature and authority.[1] This argument is an elaborate and sophisticated case for the Vedas as a *pramāṇa* (source of valid knowledge) and this chapter seeks to explicate this perspective. My discussion here focuses, in a special way, on the tradition of Advaita Vedānta. The understanding of scripture as a *pramāṇa* is neglected in the contemporary study of Hinduism, although this approach may lend a fresh perspective to the meaning and significance of sacred texts and a unique way of understanding their authority. Scripture as *pramāṇa*, is a Hindu argument which enriches our understanding of sacred texts and ought to be a prominent point of view in the contemporary discussion of the nature and authority of scripture.

One of the most important outcomes of understanding the Vedas as a source of valid knowledge, with other sources like perception and inference, is that the argument for their validity cannot be centered solely on their origin. Although Śaṅkara regards the Vedas as having their source in the infinite *brahman*, this is not the cornerstone of his argument for the authority of the texts. He does not argue often for the authority of the Vedas on the basis of *brahman*'s omniscience. His reason is that such an argument ends up hopelessly circular, since one establishes the omniscience of *brahman* from the Vedas and then the authority of the Vedas from *brahman*'s omniscience. Śaṅkara's principal and important arguments are centered on the nature of the Vedas as a source of valid knowledge. Another important consequence of defining the scripture as a *pramāṇa* is that it cannot claim exemption from being subject to the same criteria that are employed to establish the validity of other sources of knowledge.

The Nature of Valid Knowledge

Valid knowledge, according to the Advaita tradition, is knowledge that conforms to the nature of the object that one seeks to know. Knowledge does not offer the same choices like action, since actions generally present us with alternative methods for accomplishing a goal. The particular choice is dependent on human will and circumstances. If I am traveling between two cities, for example, I may have the option of choosing different routes. Valid knowledge is generated only by the application of a valid and appropriate means of knowledge, referred to as a *prāmaṇa.* A *pramāṇa*, therefore, may be understood to be a means of valid knowledge (*pramā*). Advaita recognizes six valid means of knowledge. These are perception, inference, comparison, postulation, non-cognition, and the Vedas.[2] Advaita regards the Vedas as a means of valid knowledge that functions through the instrumentality of words (*śabda*).

The cornerstone of Śaṅkara's argument for the authority of the Vedas is that the texts fulfil the criteria of being a source of valid knowledge. The Advaita tradition proposes that valid knowledge must satisfy a double criterion. First, it must inform us of a subject matter that cannot be ascertained through the operation of another means of knowledge. Second, its claims must not be contradicted by anything established through other valid sources. Novelty and noncontradiction, therefore, are considered to be the crucial characteristics of valid sources of knowledge. We will examine each criterion in turn, beginning with the novelty argument.

The Novelty of Valid Knowledge

According to Śaṅkara, the two subjects, inaccessible to all other sources of knowledge and available only through the Vedas, are *dharma* and *brahman*.[3] The knowledge of *dharma,* that is the relationship between the performance or nonperformance of prescribed ritual actions and the results which they produce, is derived from the ritual or first sections of the Vedas. These connections cannot be empirically validated. Advaita's interest, however, is primarily in the *Upaniṣads*, the last sections of the Vedas that reveal the knowledge of *brahman*.

The novelty argument suggests that the means of knowledge one selects, in any given situation, must be appropriate to object that is the focus of inquiry. In fact, it is more correct to suggest that the nature of the object to be known determines the choice of the means of knowledge. Each sense organ, for example, grants us a unique perceptual experience. The color of an object may be known only through the eyes, while the organ of smell reveals its odor. There is a logical interdependence, therefore, between the means of knowledge and the nature of the entity to be known. The cornerstone of Śaṅkara's case for the *Upaniṣads* as the valid means for knowing *brahman* is grounded in the nature of *brahman.*

In making the case for the validity and appropriateness of the words of the *Upaniṣads* as the means of knowing *brahman,* Śaṅkara repeatedly discusses the reasons why other means are inapplicable. He explains the inability of sense perception to know *brahman.* Each sense organ is naturally capable of revealing a quality that is appropriate to its own nature. Sound, sensation, form, taste and scent are their respective spheres of functioning. *Brahman,* however, remains unknowable through any of these because of its uniqueness. *Brahman* has neither sound, touch, form, taste, nor smell, and is therefore outside the domain of these sense organs. A *brahman* that is apprehended through the senses is, from the Advaita viewpoint, a contradiction, since such a *brahman* will be a limited object. Śaṅkara rejects the claim that there is a contradiction in the *Bhagavadgītā*'s denial of *brahman* as both *sat* (existent) and *asat* (non-existent) by interpreting these terms to signify the non-availability of *brahman* as an object of sense knowledge.

> No; for being beyond the reach of the senses, it is not an object of consciousness accompanied with the idea of either (existence or non-existence). That thing indeed which can be perceived by the senses, such as a pot, can be an object of consciousness accompanied with the idea of non-existence. Since, on the other hand, the Knowable is beyond the reach of the senses and as such can be known solely through that instrument of knowledge that is called *sabda.* It cannot be, like a pot, etc., an object of consciousness accompanied with the idea of either (existence or non-existence) and is therefore not said to be '*sat*' or '*asat*.'[4]

In addition to the inherent limitation of the sense organs in knowing an object that is without sense qualities, there is also the impossibility of objectifying *brahman.* The process of empirical knowledge involves a distinction between subject and object, the knower and the known. We know things by making them objects of our awareness and, in this way, they are available for scrutiny and analysis. Knowledge of an object presupposes the subject, the knower. *Brahman,* however, is the ultimate subject. As awareness, it illumines everything, and the entire universe, including mind, body, and sense organs, is its object. It is logically impossible for the subject to become an object; there will be no subject to know the subject as an object.

> Even in the state of ignorance, when one sees something, through what instrument should one know that owing to which all this is known? For the instrument of knowledge itself falls under the category of objects. The knower may desire to know, not about itself, but about objects. As fire does not burn itself, so the self does not know itself and the knower can have no knowledge of a thing that is not its object. Therefore, through what instrument should one know the Knower owing to which this universe is known and who else should know it?[5]

If perception is unsuitable for providing us with the knowledge of *brahman*, are any of the other four methods of knowing competent? Śaṅkara's view is that these sources are more or less dependent on perception for their data and are not helpful in those areas where perception has no access. Inferential knowledge, for example, is derived from discerning the invariable relation between a thing inferred and the ground from which the inference is made. *Brahman*, however, is not invariably related to any apprehensible or differentiating qualities that can form the ground of an inference. It is impossible, therefore, to infer anything about the absolute *brahman*.

Noncontradiction and Valid Knowledge

The second criterion for valid knowledge is noncontradiction. This criterion, as far as Advaita is concerned, is the fundamental and the crucial test of truth. An invalid proposition can be refuted on the grounds of being contradicted. The principle of noncontradiction implies that a claim is generally held to be valid until it is falsified by another valid means of knowledge. In Śaṅkara's view, one valid source of knowledge does not and should not contradict another.

Śaṅkara does not deny the capacity of sources like perception and inference to produce valid knowledge in their respective spheres in the world. He states, in fact, that practical affairs will become impossible if the recognized sources of valid knowledge are regarded as fundamentally perverse.

> If you challenge the validity of an inference of the kind not based on a causal relation, all of our activities, including eating and drinking, would be impossible, which you certainly do not desire. We see in life that people who have experienced that hunger and thirst, for instance, are appeased by eating and drinking, proceed to adopt these means, expecting similar results; all these would be impossible. As a matter of

> fact, however, people who have the experience of eating and drinking infer, on the ground of similarity, that their hunger and thirst would be appeased if they ate and drank again, and proceed to act accordingly.[6]

These sources, however, are not capable of conveying valid knowledge about the ultimate nature of reality.

The Limits of the Vedas

The nature of the Vedas as a source of valid knowledge, along with the criteria of novelty and noncontradiction, imply that the texts have a very limited sphere of authority. As noted earlier, the Vedas are a *pramāṇa* for the specific knowledge of *dharma* and *brahman*, which is unavailable through any other sources. It is not authoritative where it reveals information that one may obtain or has obtained from another source of valid knowledge.

It is not the primary function of the Vedas to disclose matters within the range of human experience, ascertainable through our ordinary means of knowledge such as perception and inference. If a Veda statement contradicts a well-established fact of our everyday experience, it cannot be considered authoritative because such a matter would be outside its authority. Śaṅkara remarkably admits this truth.

> *Śruti* is an authority only in matters not perceived by means of ordinary instruments of knowledge such as *pratyakṣa* or immediate perception; -i.e., it is an authority as to the mutual relation of things as means to ends, but not in matters lying within the range of *pratyakṣa*; indeed, *śruti* is intended as an authority only for knowing what lies beyond the range of human knowledge.... A hundred *śrutis* may declare that fire is cold or that it is dark; still they possess no authority in this matter.[7]

If *śruti* did describe fire as being cold or dark, we would be obliged to construe its meaning figuratively, since the purpose of the Veda is not to create anything new or to reverse the nature of anything. The texts are fundamentally revelatory in purpose and are concerned with expressing things as they are.

> Things in the world are known to possess certain fixed characteristics such as grossness or fineness. By citing them as examples, the scripture seeks to tell us about some other thing which does not contradict them. They would not cite an example from life if they wanted to convey an idea of something contradictory to it. Even if they did, it would be to no purpose, for the example would be different from the thing to be explained. You cannot prove that fire is cold, or that the sun does not shine, even by citing a hundred examples, for the facts would already be known to be otherwise through another means of knowledge. And one means

> of knowledge does not contradict another, for it only tells us about those things that cannot be known by another means. Nor can scripture speak about an unknown thing without having recourse to conventional words and their meanings.[8]

The Advaita tradition is very specific about some of the topics that are not authoritatively revealed in the scripture. It is not the purpose of scripture, for example, to inform us of history, religious biography or about the order and details of the creation of the world. A religion may offer an interpretation of the meaning of history, but the facts of history are not the authoritative concern of religion. It is not also the concern of scripture to describe the nature of the human being with regard to such characteristics that are available for observation.

The Fruitfulness of Knowledge

The role of *pramāṇa* in Advaita is not, however, merely to inform us, without consequences, of the nature of *brahman*. The knowledge of *brahman* aims to resolve a fundamental human problem of ignorance (*avidyā*) and the case for the *pramāṇa* is integrally connected with its ability to accomplish this purpose. Although it is not offered as a formal characteristic of valid knowledge, like novelty and noncontradiction, Śaṅkara repeatedly alludes to the fruitfulness and adequacy of the sentences of the *Upaniṣad*s as an additional argument for their validity. How can words be a fruitful and adequate solution to a problem? It depends, of course, on the nature of the problem and this argument is also at the heart of the Advaita claim.

The case for the adequacy of the words of the *Upaniṣad*s is based on the argument that these words are not required to create *brahman* or even to prove the existence of *brahman*. Words alone cannot bring a non-existent entity into existence and, in this case, they are not required to do so. There are several important and interesting discussions in Śaṅkara's commentaries that are relevant to this issue.

In his introduction to the Brahmasūtra, Śaṅkara raises an objection to the superimposition argument.[9] The objector's view is that superimposition is possible only on something that is available for sense perception. In the erroneous apprehension of a rope for a snake, for example, at least the outline of the rope is seen. How can anything, however, be superimposed on *brahman* that is not an object of perception? In his reply to this objection, Śaṅkara contends that even though *brahman* is not an object of perception, it is not entirely unknown and wrong understanding is possible.

> The Self is not absolutely beyond apprehension, because it is apprehended as the content of the concept "I", and because the Self, opposed to the non-Self, is well known in the world as an immediately perceived (i.e., self-revealing) entity.[10]

Elsewhere, the objector asks whether *brahman* is known or unknown. The point of the query here is that if *brahman* is known, there is no need for a means of knowledge or for an inquiry to ascertain its nature. If, on the other hand, *brahman* is entirely unknown, that is not even the object of a desire to know, then it cannot become the subject for any kind of inquiry. Śaṅkara denies that *brahman* is entirely unknown.

> Besides, the existence of *brahman* is well known from the fact of Its being the Self of all; for everyone feels that his Self exists, and he never feels, "I do not exist." Had there been no general recognition of the existence of the Self, everyone would have felt, "I do not exist." And that Self is *brahman*.[11]

If *brahman* as the self is known, one may ask, is not inquiry into the words of Vedas redundant? Śaṅkara's response is to suggest that the knowledge which we possess, is only of a general nature and the true and distinctive nature of the self remains unknown. This lack of specific knowledge is the cause, according to Śankara, of different and conflicting views about the nature of the *atmā*

In fact, wrong understanding occurs only where knowledge is of a general nature and lacks specificity. In the famous rope-snake analogy, an object is perceived as existing, but its particular nature is incorrectly ascertained. The qualities of the snake are then attributed to the rope. In the case of the self, that "I exist" and "I know" are self-revelatory. Upon this existence, and awareness, the limited qualities of the body, sense organs, and mind are wrongly attributed, and the self is taken to be mortal and finite. In other words, the qualities of the non-self are, through ignorance, erroneously superimposed on the self.

Clearly, from Śaṅkara's standpoint, the problem does not involve the knowledge of an entirely unknown, or remote *brahman*. It is one of incomplete and erroneous knowledge of an ever-available and self-manifesting entity. The function of the words of the *Upaniṣad*s lies in the negation of attributes imposed through ignorance on *brahman*. The *Upanishads* do not reveal an unknown being. They impart correct knowledge about a self that is immediately available but whose nature is misunderstood.

One of the important reasons for emphasizing the immediate availability of the self, and clarifying the nature of the ignorance pertaining to it, is that it establishes the possibility of the words of the *Upaniṣads* giving rise to direct and immediate knowledge. The challenge is not one of creating anything new, but of understanding what is always available but misunderstood. Śaṅkara accepts that the knowledge derived through words is not fruitful if the object about which it informs is not yet in existence or not immediately available. If the object is available but misapprehended, like *brahman*, correct knowledge through the words of a valid source is adequate.

> The attainment of the Self cannot be, as in the case of things other than It, the obtaining of something not obtained before, for here there is no difference between the person attaining and the object attained. Where the Self has to obtain something other than Itself, the Self is the attainer and the non-Self is the object attained. This, not being already attained, is separated from acts such as producing and is to be attained by the initiation of a particular action with the help of auxiliaries. And the attainment of something new is transitory, being due to desire and action that are themselves the product of a false notion, like the birth of a son etc. in a dream. By the very fact of Its being the Self, It is not separated by acts such as producing. But although it is always attained, It is separated by ignorance only.[12]

The above argument is the basis for Śaṅkara's important distinction between action and knowledge. Action is a correct and appropriate solution where the problem involved is the accomplishment of something unaccomplished. Knowledge, on the other hand, is adequate for the accomplishment of the already accomplished, and it is clear from Śaṅkara's analysis that he sees the attainment of *brahman* to be of this kind.

In opposition to those exegetes who contend that only scriptural injunctions inculcating the performance of acceptable acts and prohibitions instituting restraint from forbidden actions are direct and independent in authority, Śaṅkara argues for the independent authority of the sentences of the *Upaniṣads*.[13]

Śaṅkara does not accept that sentences cannot have a factual referent or significance. He points out that even though a sentence might have its ultimate purport in initiating some activity, it does not thereby cease to communicate valid factual information. Even as a person travelling to a destination perceives the existence of leaves and grass at the side of the road, a statement might have its aim in activity, but its factual content is not thereby invalidated. Replying to the claim that mere factual statements that neither persuade us into activity nor dissuade us from it are fruitless, Śaṅkara contends that,

> the test of the authority or otherwise of a passage is not whether it states a fact or an action, but its capacity to generate certain and fruitful knowledge. A passage that has this is authoritative and one that lacks it is not.[14]

He never tires of affirming the independent fruitfulness of the *Upaniṣad* sentences. These sentences, by helping us to understand the self, release us from the sorrow of taking ourselves to be incomplete and finite beings.

> Is or is not certain and fruitful knowledge generated by passages setting forth the nature of the Self, and if so, how can they lose their authority? Do you not see the result of knowledge in the removal of evils which are the root of transmigration, such as ignorance, grief, delusion, and fear? Or do you not hear those hundreds of Upanishadic texts such as, "Then what delusion and what grief can there be for the one who sees unity?"[15]

Śaṅkara points also to the transformed life of the knower of *brahman* as further evidence of the fruitfulness of knowledge gained through the words of the *Upaniṣad*.

> For one who has realized the state of unity of the Self and *brahman*, it cannot be proved that his mundane life continues just as before; for this contradicts the knowledge of the unity of *brahman* and the Self arising from the Vedas which are a valid means of knowledge. From noticing the fact that a man can have sorrow, fear, etc. as a result of identifying himself with the body etc., it does not follow that this very man will have sorrow etc., contingent on false ignorance, even when his self-identification with the body etc., ceases after realization of the unity of *brahman* and the Self, arising from the Vedas which are a valid means of knowledge.[16]

In Śaṅkara, the argument for the validity of the Vedas as source of knowledge is constructed on the basis of novelty, noncontradiction and fruitfulness. The argument for novelty ensures that the Vedas are not redundant and do not merely inform us of what can be known from other sources. Noncontradiction is concerned with truth and validates the correspondence between the claims of the texts and reality. Valid knowledge corresponds to the object that one seeks to know and is not subject to the choices of the knower. Fruitfulness is not an independent criterion of valid knowledge. Combined with novelty and noncontradiction, however, it points to the pragmatic nature of the Vedas to liberate through the dispelling of ignorance about the self. Śaṅkara's case for the authority of the Vedas, therefore, rests on arguments demonstrating a connection between the nature of *brahman*, the inappropriateness of traditional ways of knowing (viz. perception and inference), and the appropriateness of the words of the *Upaniṣads*. The knowledge gained from these words about the nature of the self is adequate since the problem is one of misunderstanding the self that is always present and available.

Is the Argument Circular?

We must ask, however, whether the Advaita claim for the Vedas as the valid source of our knowledge about *brahman* does not also have a circular character of its own. In other words, the Vedas inform us of the nature of *brahman* and also of their authoritative status as the *pramāṇa* for *brahman*. We learn from the Vedas that *brahman* does not have any quality that may be discerned by the sense organs and that it is the eternal subject that cannot be objectified. Words, therefore, are the only medium of knowledge. Is this different from any other claim that can neither be refuted nor verified? If no other *pramāṇa* is applicable to inquiry into the nature of *brahman*, how do we make any extra-Veda evaluation?

This is an important question that cannot be left unaddressed and there are, at least, two significant observations to be made. The first is an argument that we encountered earlier. The definition of the Vedas as a source of valid knowledge means that its teachings cannot contradict what we know about the nature of reality through other valid sources. The Vedas, in this sense, are subject to the critique and assessment of other sources and cannot propound contradictory or untrue claims. Second, and perhaps most important, Advaita welcomes the use of other sources into the inquiry about the nature of *brahman*, even while admitting the authority of the Vedas. The reason is that *brahman* is available and not outside of human experience. As Śaṅkara puts it, "the existence of *brahman* is well known from the fact of It being the Self of all; for everyone feels that his Self exists, and he never feels, 'I do not exist.' Had there been no general recognition of the existence of the Self, everyone would have felt, 'I do not exist.' And that Self is Brahman."[17] The matter for inquiry is the nature of the self and not its existence, and such inquiry is open, therefore, to a role for other sources of knowledge. Śaṅkara admits that this is not the case where other teachings of the Vedas are concerned. In the case of Vedic instructions and injunctions for the performance of specific rites and rituals, there is no role for other sources of knowledge. The results of these rituals will be realized in the future and are not available for immediate inquiry. The logical connection between a particular ritual and its result is not obvious and does not lend itself to inquiry through other sources. The claim therefore, that *brahman* is a unique reality, to be known by a unique means of knowledge, cannot be treated as being identical to religious claims that cannot be verified or refuted.

The Unity of Knowledge

Noncontradiction, as we have seen, is a fundamental characteristic of valid knowledge in Advaita. This places the scripture in the wider stream of discourse about the nature of reality and is opposed to the compartmentalization of human knowledge. A belief or proposition that is contradicted loses its validity. If a religious teaching contradicts a well-established fact of experience, it cannot be considered authoritative. You cannot prove, Śaṅkara said famously, that fire is cold or that the sun does not shine, by citing sentences from scripture. These are facts already established by other authoritative sources of knowledge and a scripture cannot reverse facts. If contradictions occur between different sources of knowledge, earnest inquiry is necessary for the resolution of these, and theologians must welcome and be active participants in such discussions. Advaita does not allow us to ignore science or to irrationally claim that the findings of science are false because these contradict scripture. Religious claims that are refuted by valid sources of knowledge cannot be professed in ways suggesting that such contradictions do not matter. Religion cannot claim epistemological privilege and be sheltered from wider engagement with the growing body of knowledge about our universe and life. Traditions ought not to fear truth, whatever its source. The approach helps to overcome the sharp dichotomies between diverse methodologies for the study of religion. The range of discussion partners in the commentaries of classical exponents, like Śaṅkara, is exemplary and ought to encourage even greater inclusivity.

What the Advaita tradition speaks of as the criterion of noncontradiction requires that we continuously pursue coherence between religious teachings and knowledge of the world gained through other valid sources. The pursuit of such coherence, whether in hermeneutical debates between rival interpretations, or rival worldviews, were conducted on the basis of shared and public principles of reasoning and inquiry.

The view that each *pramāṇa* has a unique sphere of authority has helped the Hindu tradition to avoid the sorts of conflict between religion and the empirical and behavioral sciences which have hampered constructive dialogue between religion and these disciplines. Religion ought not to claim authority in those fields of inquiry where its methods and sources are inappropriate. At the same time, the Advaita tradition calls for a similar acknowledgement of the limits of empirical modes of inquiry.

The understanding of scripture as a *pramāṇa* enables us also to employ the tools of contemporary historical critical methods of inquiry to study scripture, while affirming the authoritative significance of the texts. Here also, the criteria of novelty and noncontradiction become very important. For every teaching in the Vedas, we may indeed ask two fundamental questions. First, is this teaching novel or can it be known through another source? If it is something that can be known through another *pramāṇa*, then the Vedas are not the authority. Second, does it contradict any truths established by other valid sources? If it does, then such Vedic sentences are not authoritative and we may have to find other ways of understanding them.

Pramāṇa, Caste and Liberation

Let me conclude by highlighting one of the very important ways in the which the Advaita understanding of the Vedas as a source of valid knowledge, has become meaningful in my work to construct a Hindu theology of liberation.

Let us take the traditional argument for hereditary occupation, which is that human beings are qualified by birth for different occupations and must be treated differently. What are the grounds for this argument?

The authority of other *pramāṇas*, like perception and inference, challenge the claim that birth decisively determines one's occupational aptitude and competence. It is a well-known fact that there is no necessary correlation between birth in a particular family and one's qualification for a particular kind of work. The availability of opportunities, educational and economic, is critical in determining work choices. Any argument, therefore, based on scripture, that birth qualifies a person for particular occupations is refuted by empirical evidence.

This is one of the arguments offered by the great Dalit leader B. R. Ambedkar, in his response to Gandhi, who supported hereditary occupations. Ambedkar was contesting traditional claims with hard evidence.

> When can a calling be deemed to have become an ancestral calling so as to make it binding on a man? Must a man follow his ancestral calling even if it does not suit his capacities, even when it has ceased to be profitable? Must a man live by his ancestral calling even if he finds it to be immoral?[18]

The Advaita view, as we clarified, is that if scripture contradicts a well-established fact of everyday experience, it cannot be considered authoritative because such a matter is outside its authoritative sphere. The purpose of scripture is only to inform us of matters that cannot be known through conventional ways of knowing. There are valid empirical methods for determining human occupational abilities. This is not a matter that is outside the sphere of perception and inference. If the prescription of occupational choices is outside the authoritative concern of the Vedas, then all such efforts, wherever occurring, must be understood as humanly authored systems of thought and practice, that are subject to interrogation and change. In a similar way, arguments about physical purity and impurity cannot be justified by appeal to the Vedas since such claims can be refuted empirically by establishing that there is no difference in the matter that makes up different bodies. Such claims are not connected with the central purpose of the scripture to instruct about *brahman*. Scripture is not authoritative if it reveals anything that is contradicted by the evidence of other valid sources of knowledge and it is clear that the fundamental premises of the hierarchical ordering of human beings, exemplified by caste, have no empirical justification.

References

1 Vedānta is a general term used to identify those traditions that look to the *Upaniṣads,* or the final sections of the Vedas, as an authoritative source of knowledge. Advaita (not-two) is a nondualistic Vedānta tradition. It looks to a line of distinguished teachers for the interpretation of these texts and for the transmission of its teachings. The most distinguished among these is Śaṅkara, who wrote extensive commentaries on the *Upaniṣads*, the *Bhagavadgītā* and the *Brahmasūtra* and who is credited with the legacy of the finest systematic exposition of Advaita.

2 The technical term used for the Vedas in this context is *śabdapramāṇa* or words as a valid source of knowledge.

3 See BSBh 2.1.6.

4 BGBh 13:16

5 BUBh 2.4.14

6 BUBh 4.3.6.

7 BGBh 18:66. *Śruti* (that which is heard) is a term for the Vedas, calling attention to its oral reception as revelation and its transmission from teacher to student.

8 BUBh 2.I.20

9 In Advaita, superimposition (*adhyāsa*) refers to the error of attributing qualities to an object which it does not possess. The classic example is the error of mistaking a rope for a snake, where the remembered qualities of a snake are wrongly imposed on a rope. The error is corrected by right knowledge.

10 BSBh Introduction

11 BSBh 1.1.1

12 BUBh 1.4.7

13 Pūrva Mīmāṁsā, an ancient school of Vedic exegesis, contends that the Vedas are only authoritative in matters of *dharma.* For Advaita, the Vedas are authoritative for both *dharma* and *brahman.*

14 BUBh 1.4.7

15 BSBh. 1.4.7

16 BSBh 1.1.4

17 BSBh 1.1.1

18 Ambedkar, *Annihilation of Caste*, 343.

CHAPTER THREE

HINDU SPIRITUALITY

WHAT IS SPIRITUALITY?

For the purpose of the discussion, I adopt the working definition of spirituality offered by Roger Haight. "Spirituality consists in the way persons or groups live their lives in the face of what they consider ultimately important or real."[1] My emphasis here is on the normative dimension of spirituality. I am concerned less with how Hindus actually live their lives and more with how they ought to do so, given the tradition's teachings about the nature of the ultimate. In his discussion with Roger Haight, Paul Knitter criticizes Haight's definition as being too broad.[2] Buddhists, according to Knitter, begin not with ultimate reality, but with the fundamental problem of ignorance (*avidyā*). The Buddhist emphasis is on the practice necessary "to get in touch" with ultimate reality or one's Buddha-nature. In this discussion, I deploy the term in both senses. It includes the way to discovering ultimate reality as well as the implications of this discovery for our lives in the world. Spirituality includes what we do to overcome *avidyā* and the transformation that ensues in our way of being. I am not proposing any sharp distinction between spirituality and religion. I concur with Haight and Knitter in thinking of religion as referring to the "socially organized ways of being spiritual in community." Spirituality refers to the fundamental teachings and practices, the deepest theological dimensions, that define such a community.

In light of the tremendous diversity of Hindu traditions, it is more appropriate to speak of spirituality in the plural. Each tradition has its unique understanding of the nature of the ultimate, prescribes a distinctive path to liberation, and specifies its understanding of the implications of liberation for our lives. My aim here is not to homogenize these traditions. While I highlight certain shared features, my analysis is particularly influenced by the nondualism of Advaita Vedānta.

The Problem of Greed

The *Bhagavadgītā*, the battlefield conversation between the teacher, Krishna, and his disciple, Arjuna, is regarded as one of the three pillars of the Hindu Vedānta traditions. The other two are the *Upaniṣads*, which are the concluding dialogues of the Vedas, and the Brahmasūtras, a summary of the *Upaniṣads* attributed to an ancient teacher, Bādārāyaṇa.

In the second chapter of the *Bhagavadgītā*, Arjuna asks his first substantial theological question. This is not the first time he speaks in the text. His earlier words described his emotional and mental confusion about choosing to fight the war or withdraw from the battlefield. In 2:54, however, he formulates a theological question: "What is your definition," he asks his teacher, "of a wise person?" "How does such a person speak, sit, conduct himself in the world?"[3]

Krishna's answer is as profound as it is surprising. Disregarding Arjuna's request for visible, external characteristics (one can pretend, after all, to be wise by the cultivation of certain mannerisms!), Krishna speaks of an inward transformation and disposition. A wise person, explains Krishna in 2:55, is one who is free from greed as a consequence of discovering contentment in the fullness of the self (*ātmā*).

Krishna's words here and throughout the *Bhagavadgītā* are chosen carefully. He speaks of the wise person as being free from all forms of greed (*sarvān kāmān*). This is an important reminder to us of all the multiple expressions of greed in our personal lives and in our corporate and community lives. Greed is commonly identified only with the desire for wealth and the many objects of conspicuous or visible consumption that wealth affords. In thinking about the multiple expressions of greed about which Krishna speaks, we must include also the greed for power, for fame, and for sense gratification.

I want to make special mention of two manifestations of greed that are not often identified, but which are at the root of much violence, historically and in contemporary life. The first is the greed to possess, dominate and exploit other human beings for one's own ends and interests. This greed is an underlying cause of patriarchy and violence against women. Gender greed, if I may so describe it, treats women as male property, as existing only to serve male needs, who deserve to be punished and even deprived of life, when they fail to do so. It is a greed that objectifies and instrumentalizes women, treating them as male commodities.

The second form of greed, also a source of great suffering, is the obsession to have everyone believe and think as we do. It is the desire for uniformity and homogeneity, concealing a fear and anxiety of difference. Whether in the name of political ideology or religion, and sometimes both are inseparable, this compulsion is at the root of great suffering across time and place.

As the dialogue in the *Bhagavadgītā* progresses, Arjuna continues to question his teacher. His question at the end of the third chapter (3:36) and Krishna's answer are also revealing. "What is it," asks Arjuna, "that drives a human being to commit evil?" "It is greed," answers Krishna, "it is anger, the all-consuming and great evil; the enemy that is present here." We should not understand Krishna to be saying that every instance of wrongdoing may be traced back to greed. I think he is speaking here of greed as a primary and fundamental cause, and not the only cause.

Krishna's answer to Arjuna's question in chapter three sheds light on his earlier answer in chapter two about the character of the wise person. It is now clear why he chose to speak of the wise one as free from greed. He identified freedom from greed as the distinguishing feature of spirituality and wisdom because it is the principal cause of harm to self and to others. It is the adversary that is always present with us. Krishna's language is powerful and suggestive. The *Bhagavadgītā* dialogue is on a battlefield and the enemy, for Arjuna, is the warrior standing across from him on the opposite side. His entire life had been a training for battle with such an enemy. Krishna wants to draw his attention to a greater enemy, one that is invisible, much closer, and difficult to overcome. It is the enemy that is the cause of the battle at hand and of future battles as well.

Krishna's description of greed in 3:39 as an "insatiable fire (*duṣpūreṇa analena*)" helps us to identify its essential nature and to distinguish greed from need. The defining characteristic of greed is its insatiability. Whatever its object, be it power, fame, or wealth, one can never have enough. Greed makes of life a race without a finishing line. It distorts reality, fuels anxiety and disposes us to see other human beings only as rivals who threaten our self-worth.

In thinking about the problem of greed, however, it is important that we do not see it only as an individual human problem. Greed also finds expression in institutional and corporate structures and is transmitted culturally. Think, for example, of the problem of corruption across our world. Greed subverts economic growth and development. Effective legislation and policies, rigorously enforced, are needed to control and limit the harm to the public good that is caused by greed. Even legislation has its limits in the constant battle with human ingenuity fueled by greed. Legislation to control the institutional expressions of greed in the public sphere is indispensable, but the enduring solution is formation of good and ethically responsible human beings, committed to public good. This, for me, is one of the primary tasks of spirituality.

Greed and the Quest for Self-Worth

With the teachings of the *Bhagavadgītā*, we have identified greed as a primary cause of harm to self and others. We have also identified freedom from greed as a primary fruit of spirituality. We need now to step back and ask fundamental questions of the Hindu tradition. What is the origin of greed? Is it symptomatic of a deeper human problem? What is the fuel that sustains the fire of greed?

Hindu spirituality offers what I describe as an empirical answer to this question—an answer that is not speculative, but recognizable in human experience. If we look for the root of greed, we will find it in a deep sense of self-inadequacy or incompleteness, an uncertainty about one's own value; an inner emptiness, dissatisfaction. It is what the social anthropologist, Ernst Becker, speaks of as the "struggle for self-esteem" or "the desire to be 'an object of primary value.'"[4] The urge to know that one counts, that one has value, and that one's existence matters, is special to us as human beings. It is the gift and burden of our self-consciousness. Human beings are distinguished from other species by a heightened self-consciousness, but this allows also for the experience of inadequacy and the comparison of ourselves with others. This anxiety about self-worth is not one, as far as we know, that we share with another species. Without self-worth, we cannot live fulfilling and meaningful lives.

The urge to overcome the gnawing sense of self-inadequacy and to achieve adequacy of being finds expression in multifarious desires. The insatiable quest for wealth, beyond the decent satisfaction of one's needs, is explicable by the fact that wealth acquisition is a culturally acceptable way of seeking to add self-worth and to overcome the sense of self-lack. The same is true of our preoccupation with the gain of fame or power.

The tragic nature of the quest for self-acceptance and self-worth through pursuits such as pleasure, wealth, fame and power, as attested in the experiences of human beings across cultures and times, is that such gains consistently fail to satisfy and leave us wanting. Every finite gain and experience, however, whether it is sense pleasure, fame, power or wealth, results in a short-lived sense of well-being, but the sense of want persists.

There are many reasons for this. Paradoxically, we can never have enough of that which we do not really want. Since we are in search of self-worth and not really after wealth, fame or power as ends in themselves, their gain will not solve our problem. The philosopher of religion, Huston Smith, summarized the understanding of Hindu spirituality very accurately.

> While it is not true to say that men cannot get enough money, fame and power, it is true to say that men cannot get enough of these things when they want them greedily, when they make them the supreme forces of their lives. These are not the things men really want, and man can never get enough of what he does not really want.[5]

Any value attributed to oneself through gains such as wealth, power and fame, is relative and dependent on others enjoying less or on the unequal distribution of these goods. This means that the self-worth that we grant to ourselves depends on unfavorable comparisons with others. In the case of wealth, for example, we believe that our self-worth increases when our assets are worth more than those in the group used for comparison and diminishes when these assets decline. The consequence is a sense of anxiety, fear and discomfort. We proclaim our self-worth only in relation to the diminished worth of others, with tragic consequences across history.

Hindu spirituality, in its most profound sense, begins with this understanding of the human predicament. Religious belief and practice that have as their main purpose helping us achieve power and wealth in this world do not address this fundamental human predicament. This is not an argument for religious indifference to poverty or powerlessness. There is too much of greed centered religious practice that simply legitimizes human greed in all of its manifestations. Religious practice that reduces the divine to an instrument in the service of human greed does not transform us and does not create a compassionate and caring society.

Freedom from Greed

If greed originates from a universal human need for self-worth, how is this need addressed by Hindu spirituality? What answer has the tradition given to this most fundamental of human needs?

To clarify the tradition's answer, I want to share two illustrations used by the famous Hindu theologian, Śaṅkara (7th century). The first comes from his commentary on the *Bṛhadāraṇyaka Upaniṣad* (2.1.20). Here Śaṅkara tells the story of a prince, who is heir to his father's throne. He is unfortunately separated from his parents and raised in the home of a family of bird-catchers. Ignorant of his princely status, he thought of himself as a bird-catcher's son and learned to trap birds. A kind person, knowing of the boy's royal identity, found him and explained to him that he was not a bird-catcher, but a prince. As a consequence, the boy gave up his false understanding and reclaimed his true and original one. In his second example, taken from Śaṅkara's commentary on the *Chāndogya Upaniṣad* (6.14.2), he tells of a person who is forcibly seized and taken away from his beloved home, a place of happiness and security. He is blindfolded and left in the wilderness. Lost in this place of desolation, he cries out for help to find his way home. A kind person hears his cries, removes his blindfold and shows him the way back to his home.

These two illustrations, from the teacher Śaṅkara, have common themes. In both cases, something precious is lost or forgotten. In the first case, a boy does not know that he is a prince and settles for the life of a bird-catcher. In the second, a person loses his home, his place of peace and comfort, and is left to wander in the wilderness. Again, in both cases, what is forgotten or lost, could be and is recovered: the boy learns that he is a prince and the lost person finds his home. The recovery of what is precious is made possible with the help of a compassionate person.

In a similar way, the fundamental insight of Hindu spirituality is that the valued self for which every human being yearns, the adequate self that we wish to become and for which we search in vain through multifarious desires, is the self that we are. The full self that we want to become is our true intrinsic nature. The prince is still a prince, even though he thought he was a bird-catcher; the home the person longed for was still there and he just needed instructions to make his way back to it. In both cases, a certain kind of ignorance had to be overcome.

The truth that each one is a full being, is at the heart of Hindu spirituality. It is the teaching articulated in a well-known sentence of the *Upaniṣads—"That Thou Art (Tat Tvam Asi)"*—repeated twelve times by the teacher to his student in the sixth chapter of the *Chāndogya Upaniṣad*. In this sentence, "that" refers to the full being, the one being that constitutes the ontological nature of all beings, the indivisible one present at the heart of all beings.

In one of the finest teaching moments in the *Upaniṣads*, the *Chāndogya* (chapter six) teacher, Aruni, helps his son, Śvetaketu, to understand this truth by giving him a practical exercise. Aruni asks Śvetaketu to bring him the fruit of a tall and spreading banyan tree. Śvetaketu fetches the fruit and brings it before his father.

> "Break it," requested his father
> "It is broken," answered Śvetaketu
> "What do you see there?" asked his father

"These are very fine seeds," replied Śvetaketu
"Break one of these," requested his father
"It is broken," said Śvetaketu
"What do you see there?" asked his father
"Nothing at all," answered Śvetaketu

By serially breaking the seeds, Śvetaketu arrives at a point where he could not divide the seed any further. "My dear son," responds Aruni, "that finest essence which you do not see, from that essence this great banyan tree arises. Have faith, my son. That which is the finest essence, this whole world has for its self. That is the Truth. That is the Self. That Thou Art, Śvetaketu." The full self is the original nature and at the heart of every being.

Śaṅkara also illustrates the human problem and its resolution with his famous story of the tenth person. Ten students were on a pilgrimage when they encountered a flooded river. Not finding a boatman, they entered the raging waters. After reaching the opposite bank, the students decided to take a count to ensure that everyone was safe. Each one counted, and concluded that they had lost a member of the group—the tenth person. A woodcutter, returning home from a long day's work, saw the disconsolate students and inquired about their problem. After listening patiently, he requested the leader to repeat his count. When the leader stopped at nine, the stranger smiled and asked, "Did you count yourself?" The students immediately understood the problem: the tenth person was found! The loss occurred because of ignorance, since the tenth person had always been present. The finding was an awakening to this truth.

In a similar way, we have concluded wrongly about ourselves, without proper inquiry, and assumed that we are incomplete. We then spend our entire lives in a futile search for fullness of self. Through the instruction of scripture and teacher, we discover and understand that the self *(ātmā)*, which we just assumed to be incomplete, is, in fact, identical in nature with the full and limitless *brahman*.

Understanding this truth about oneself, internalizing it, and allowing it to transform one's life are at the heart of Hindu spirituality. Greed is overcome only when one discovers an inner plenitude, the fullness of the self. Hindu spirituality does not promise to free us from ageing, or ill-health; it does not promise that every one of our desires will be fulfilled, or that we will altogether avoid unpleasant experiences. What it does offer is a transformed understanding of self that leads to a condition of psychological health and well-being. This is living liberation—a life lived from the fullness of being and not from greed and smallness of self.

In our discussion so far, we considered the theological foundations of Hindu spirituality focusing on the problem of greed and its roots in a deep sense of lack or inadequacy. The central and liberating insight of Hindu spirituality is that the self of each human being is full and whole. The self that is whole is one, and present identically in all beings. One comes to know oneself as the self of all. *Īśa Upaniṣad* (6) relates this knowledge of the identity of *brahman* in all to freedom from hate.

> One who sees all beings in the self alone and the self in all beings, feels no hate by virtue of that understanding.[6]

Implications of Liberation for Life in the World

What are the implications of Hindu spirituality for our lives in families and communities? Here I wish to highlight ten outcomes.

First, the focus of Hindu spirituality is life in this world, here and now. The goal of Hindu spirituality is *mokṣa*, or liberation from wrong understanding of oneself. This end is to be attained here and now. The fruit of Hindu spirituality does not await the death of the body. The ideal is living liberation, that is a transformed life in this world. Too often, Hindu spirituality is described in ways that seem to suggest a turning away from the world or escape from the cycle of birth, death and rebirth. It is important to emphasize, therefore, that Hindu spirituality does not culminate in the rejection of the world, but a transformed way of being in the world; a way of being in the world that is characterized by freedom from greed in its many manifestations.

For Hindu spirituality, the world itself is not problematized. The problem, as we have discussed above, is ignorance (*avidyā*). Swami Vivekananda, distinguished teacher of Hindu spirituality, expressed the wish not to be free from the world but to return to it again and again to serve God in the poor and suffering. "May I be born again and again," said Vivekananda, "and suffer thousands of miseries so that I may worship the only God that exists, the only God I believe in, the sum total of all souls— and, above all, my God the wicked, my God the miserable, my God the poor of all races, of all species, is the special object of my worship."[7] Hindu spirituality does not ask us to endure a life of suffering here in the hope of a better life in the beyond. If the full life is not gained here, it will not be gained elsewhere.

Second, if Hindu spirituality does not culminate in the renunciation of life in the world, it does not also isolate, or alienate, us from other human beings. On the contrary, it draws us into a deep unity with all. The infinite *brahman* exists equally and identically in all beings. The

Bhagavadgītā (6:29-32) speaks interchangeably of seeing oneself in all and seeing God in all.

How we see our connectedness with others depends, in large measure, on how we see ourselves. A selfish person identifies with no one but himself; everyone exists instrumentally to serve his needs. For others, the circle of identity extends to their immediate families and friends; they are moved by their joys and sorrows. For others, it may extend to the village, town, or nation. It may even stretch beyond national boundaries to include an ethnic group or religious tradition. The wider the circle of our identity, the better we reflect the insight of Hindu spirituality. Hindu spirituality culminates in a circle of identity that excludes no one. For this reason, Hindu spirituality cannot be identified narrowly with the interests of a particular nation or ethnic group. Although it has a close historical relationship with the culture of India, its essential insights are not culture-specific and it is capable of flourishing in diverse cultural locations.

It is important to clarify that the ideal of identifying oneself with all beings does not exempt one from fulfilling specific obligations. One serves the world by fulfilling the obligations of specific relationships as a parent, spouse, child, family member, or worker.

Third, a circle of identity that includes all human beings is a powerful justification for ethical responsibility in a globalized world. Hindu spirituality affirms our common humanity, grounded in the unity of self, but it is not anthropocentric. The circle of identity includes also the world of nature. The *Śvetāśvatara Upaniṣad* (4:3), speaking of *brahman* as the self of all, is inclusive in its language. "You are a woman; you are a man; you are a boy and also a girl. As an old man, you totter along with a walking stick. You are the dark blue bird, the green one with red eyes, the rain-cloud, the seasons, and the oceans. You live as one without a beginning because of your pervasiveness, you, from whom all beings are born."

Hindu spirituality enables us to overcome our alienation from the natural world. It does not confer the right to dominate, possess and make all other living beings subservient to our needs and wants. The uniqueness of the human being is to be found in our ability to discern life's unity in *brahman* and to cultivate value and reverence for all life. The challenge, however, always remains to translate theological value and insight into policy and action. A spiritual value for nature does not always find expression in good environmental practice. The Ganges, for example, which is India's most sacred river is also among the most polluted. The overcoming of greed, which is a significant fruit of Hindu spirituality, implies responsibility and moderation in our use of the world's natural resources.

Fourth, the identical presence of *brahman*, the ultimate, in all beings, is the source of the inherent dignity and equal worth of every human being. Hindu spirituality cannot give its assent or support to any social, political or cultural system founded on human inequality and injustice. This requires of us great diligence and discernment in identifying such systems and in highlighting their contradictions. To see women as inferior to men, to prefer the boy-child over the girl-child, to regard the widow as inauspicious, to mistreat the elderly, to demean and to practice violence against gay people, are all in fundamental contradiction to the meaning of Hindu spirituality.

Hindu spirituality is an antidote to our tendency to deny the personhood, worth and dignity of others. Although it is hazardous to generalize about conflicts around our world, each one having its unique causes, it is also true that opposing sides in these conflicts engage in a rhetoric of depersonalizing each other and denying common identity. The denial of the personhood of the other is a predictable and persistent feature of communities in conflict, past and present. As such, overcoming beliefs, speech and actions that demonize others, has to be part of any solution and quest for reconciliation. Hindu spirituality has much to teach about how we engage and converse with opponents across political, national or other divides.

Hindu spirituality enables us to see ourselves in the other, the one with whom we disagree and with whom we may be locked in struggle. It is difficult to dehumanize someone in whom we see ourselves. This approach was at the heart of the Gandhian philosophy and practice of nonviolent resistance (*satyāgraha*). Even in the midst of the strongest disagreements, Gandhi never sought to win support for his case by demonizing his opponent. He understood clearly that when a conflict is constructed sharply in terms of "we" and "they," victory and defeat, the doors to reconciliation and a transformed community are shut. One is left with an enemy, a defeated enemy perhaps, and the next round of the conflict is only postponed. Gandhi included the opponent in the circle of his identity. He brought vital insights from Hindu spirituality to his work in the political and social spheres. Gandhi's refusal to dehumanize others, even in the midst of conflict, is a practice from which we can all learn.

Fifth, the value that best expresses, for me, the meaning of Hindu spirituality is compassion (*dayā*). In the *Bhagavadgītā* (12:13), Krishna speaks of the ideal human being as one who has no hatred towards anyone, and who is friendly, compassionate and forgiving. Compassion flows from our understanding of life's unity and ability to see ourselves in others and others in ourselves. The measure of our growth in Hindu spirituality, is our ability to respond to the suffering of others as we may respond to our own, and to celebrate with them in joy. The best of *yogīs*, according to Krishna (6: 32), is the one who identifies with others in sorrow and in joy.

The great Hindu poet-saint, Tulasidasa, gives pride of place to compassion as an expression of spirituality, in his description of the saintly person in Rāmacaritamānas (Uttara Kāṇḍa). He describes the saint as "one who is unhappy when others are unhappy and happy when others are happy (*para duhkha duhkha sukha sukha dekhem para*)." The unmistakable connection between spirituality and compassion in the Hindu tradition underlines an important, but often overlooked, fact: the ideal of Hindu spirituality is not a life in splendid isolation and indifference, absorbed in oneself and in uncaring detachment from the world. It is deep identification with others. In the same discussion, Tulasidasa speaks of the saint as having a tender heart and as being compassionate to the poor. He is specific in identifying the poor as those in our community who must be the special recipients of concern and compassion. Compassion needs to be wedded with the pursuit of justice.

Compassion is not a mere sentiment. Its proper application requires discernment. Its practice at the individual level or in state policy requires more than good intentions. Discernment is necessary to ensure that outcomes are beneficial. There are too many examples of rightly motivated individual and state efforts failing to generate good outcomes because of improper planning and execution. In addressing any problem, compassion does not exempt us from asking critical questions: What are the underlying structural causes—economic, social or political? What are the choices in action? What are the resources necessary? What outcome is likely to yield sustainable results? In the *Bhagavadgītā* (18:20-22) Krishna commends generosity, but insists that legitimate needs are identified, the right recipients chosen, and that thought be given to the maximization of outcomes.

Sixth, while compassion flows from an inward transformation in understanding of self, it must find expression in meaningful outward action. The social or political expression of such action is what Krishna, in the *Bhagavadgītā* speaks of as *lokasaṁgraha* or the public good. Hindu spirituality must be oriented towards the public good. Krishna's insight into the relationship between spirituality and the public good is a critical one that still remains untapped in Hindu thinking, about public policy and political action.

Krishna uses the word *lokasaṁgraha* twice in the *Bhagavadgītā* (3:20; 3:25). In each case, he emphasizes the necessity of keeping one's attention on the public good in every action. Hindu spirituality requires that the public good be a factor in all human choices; it is not consistent with actions that are detrimental to the public good. A concern for the public good is what transforms and spiritualizes all commitments and obligations.

The Hindu tradition recognizes that obligations (*dharma*) are multiple and complex. These depend on one's stage in life, one's relationships, and the groups to which one belongs. As a husband, as a father, as a son, I have obligations to my wife, my children and my parents. The loving fulfillment of these obligations is an expression of the meaning of spirituality in the Hindu tradition. In meeting my personal obligations, I am required to ensure that I do so with regard for the public good. It is possible to imagine ways in which one's family loyalty could be expressed in ways that hurt the public good. In the same way, one's work in the public sector or the private sector, one's loyalty to one's nation, political party, or religious community, must be expressed in ways consistent with the public good. A narrow understanding of national loyalty with adverse effects on other nations is inconsistent with the demands of Hindu spirituality. In Hindu spirituality, the public good becomes the normative measure of the meaning of all that we do.

Seventh, Hindu spirituality is a spirituality of personal responsibility. This dimension of Hindu spirituality is emphasized most significantly in the tradition's teachings about *karma*, a vast teaching open to multiple interpretations. At its core, however, there are three important insights. First, is the fact that actions are consequential. The choices that we make in life, small and big, matter. In the interconnected web of existence, our choices have implications for us, for others and, as discussed earlier, for the common good. Spirituality offers us wisdom, values and inspiration, but the implementation of these in action is our responsibility. Second, the Hindu teaching about *karma* is associated with a worldview that includes rebirth. The opposite of life is not death, but new life. The consequences of our action are so significant that these extend beyond our current lives. Whatever one thinks about this specific claim, it is enough to appreciate that the consequences of our actions, extend beyond our lifespan. The choices that we make in our families, or in the centers of decision making in corporations and governments, do not end with our lives. Whether we are mindful of it or not, we are shaping the world for future generations. If we care, we must act thoughtfully and with a commitment to the public good. The third insight about karma is hope.

The consequence of our selfish actions, individual and corporate, can be rectified, but it may take more than a single lifetime to do it. If the consequences of our selfishness extend beyond this life, or into the distant future, remedying these consequences will also take more than one life. The essential idea here is that we are continuously making ourselves, constructing who we are individually and nationally, by our modes of thought and action. The formation of character, individually and communally, is not mysterious or inexplicable; it is constructed by repeated and habitual thought, feelings, speech and action. *Karma* is an affirmation of the freedom to become the kind of person or community that we wish to be; in this freedom, there are the seeds of hope. Hope frees us to imagine a new future that can be shaped by transformed life choices in the present.

Eighth, spirituality cannot be opposed to fact. If a religious statement or claim contradicts a well-established fact of experience, it cannot be considered authoritative. As Śaṅkara wrote in his *Bhagavadgītā* (18:66) commentary, "A hundred scriptures may declare that fire is cold or that it is dark; still they possess no authority in this matter." Spiritual teachings must be understood within the parameters of human reason and experience, and contradictions cannot go unaddressed. When contradictions occur, earnest inquiry is necessary for the resolution of these, and religious teachers must welcome and be active participants in such discussions. Spiritual teachings cannot be compartmentalized or privatized, and claim exemption from critical rational examination. Spirituality cannot claim exemption from a wider engagement with our growing body of knowledge about the universe.

Ninth, Hindu spirituality finds expression in a reverence for life. This reverence for life has its roots in our ability to discern the one limitless *brahman* present in the many. The ethical value that most eloquently expresses this reverence for life is non-injury (*ahiṁsā*), regarded in the Hindu tradition as the foremost of virtues. In his understanding and interpretation of the meaning of *ahiṁsā*, Gandhi explained that in its negative form it means abstention from injury to living beings physically or mentally. In its positive form, *ahiṁsā* also means love and compassion for all. For Gandhi, *ahiṁsā* also meant justice towards everyone and abstention from exploitation in any form. "No man," claimed Gandhi, "could be actively nonviolent and not rise against social injustice no matter where it occurred." Reverence for life and its expression in the practice of *ahimsā* must become evident not only in the great matters of war and peace, but in human relationships at every level—in our parenting practices, in the ethos of our educational institutions, in business corporations, in the character of our national debates, in our conflict resolution practices and in our healthcare institutions. No community will long endure without an intrinsic reverence for life.

Tenth, and finally, Hindu spirituality is a spirituality of hospitality. In a commencement address to his students in the *Taittirīya Upaniṣad* (1.11.1-2), the teacher advises his students as follows:

> Do not neglect your duties to *devas* and ancestors. May you become one for whom your mother is a *deva*. May you become one for whom your father is a *deva*. May you become one for whom your teacher is a *deva*. May you become one for whom the stranger (*atithi*) is a *deva*.

In the Hindu tradition, a *deva* is a being deserving of reverence, respect and honor. A *deva* is accorded hospitality and offered gifts. Generally, in the Vedas, a *deva* (radiant or shining) refers to a celestial being responsible for regulating some natural phenomena in the cosmos. They include beings like Agni (Fire), Vayu (Air), Varuna (Water) and Pṛthvī (Earth). It is quite likely that the students of the Vedas had this understanding of the word. It may have surprised these students, therefore, to hear their venerable teacher elevating their parents and teachers to this status and asking them to regard and treat them as *devas*. This was a new teaching to their ears and the teacher's progression was deliberate. He begins with biological and intimate family relationships—mother and father—moves to the teacher, and ends with the stranger.

Including the stranger is the boldest move in the *Taittirīya* text. Most of the English translations of this text render *atithi* as "guest." Although this is acceptable, it is not as bold as other possibilities. *Atithi* literally means a person who one encounters without an appointment or a time agreed upon for meeting (*tithi*). It is the unplanned and spontaneous meeting and thus more likely to occur in the encounter with a stranger. I read the text, therefore, as inviting us to regard all human beings, those with whom we share family bonds, those to whom we are indebted for the gift of knowledge, and the strangers who we encounter, as *devas*. Each is a being deserving our reverence, respect and hospitality. The stranger is not qualified in any way by religion, caste, place of origin, age, or gender. The stranger may even be without religious commitment. The stranger is deserving of our respect by the fact of one's humanity. The implications of this obligation to hospitality in Hindu spirituality has profound implications today, for our response to our fellow human beings who are forced to flee their homes because of poverty, violence and natural disasters, and who seek relief at our borders.

The core Hindu moral values that must guide our response to refugees are compassion and hospitality. It is immoral if, because of xenophobia, prejudice or calculation of our own economic benefits, we shut our hearts and our doors to those who come to us in desperate need for protection and the sustenance of life. We must ensure that concerns about security are legitimate and not excuses for racism or intolerance. This is the response required of us by the spirituality of the Hindu tradition.

References

1 See Paul Knitter and Roger Haight, *Jesus and Buddha* (Maryknoll: Orbis Books, 2015), 8.

2 Knitter and Haight, *Jesus and Buddha,* 13-15.

3 This is my paraphrasing of Arjuna's question.

4 See Ernest Becker, *The Denial of Death* (New York: Free Press, 1973), 4.

5 Huston Smith, *The Religions of Man*, 20.

6 My translation.

7 *The Complete Works of Swami Vivekananda* (abbreviated CW), 8 vols., Mayavati Memorial Edition (Calcutta: Advaita Ashrama,1964-1971). CW 5: 137

PART II
DIALOGUE

CHAPTER FOUR

HINDUS AND CHRISTIANS: CELEBRATING FRIENDSHIP AND FACING CHALLENGES WITH HOPE

A History of Friendship

The order of the words in the title of this chapter, "Hindus and Christians: Celebrating Friendship and Facing Challenges With Hope" is significant.[1] Although the differences between the Hindu and Christian traditions, doctrinal and otherwise, must not be minimized or overlooked and our challenges identified and confronted, we ought not to forget the long history of friendship between Hindus and Christians, and the relationships of mutual enrichment and learning that deserve to be noted and celebrated. To ignore or forget this history is to be unfaithful to our relationship and to deprive us of a precious memory that inspires and offers hope for our common future. The fact is that Hindus and Christians have lived as friends and neighbors on the Indian sub-continent for centuries. Hindus also live peacefully as minorities among Christians in many parts of our world, including Asia, Africa, Europe, North America, the Caribbean and Australia.

A Mutual Affection for Jesus

At the heart of this friendship on the Hindu side is a profound attraction for Jesus of Nazareth and for those who follow his path through discipleship. Quite early, in the history of this encounter, many Hindus made the difficult and problematic effort to distinguish Jesus from the institution of the Church and its doctrines. Hindus felt that the meaning of Jesus could not be limited to the historical institutions that claimed to represent him or the doctrines that sought to interpret the significance of his life.

Ram Mohan Roy

Ram Mohan Roy (1772–1833), the first Hindu to attempt a systematic study of Christianity, confessed his immense difficulty, "amidst the various doctrines, I found insisted upon in the writings of Christian authors, and in the conversation of those teachers of Christianity with whom I had the honor of holding communication."[2] In 1820, Roy published a small work entitled *The Precepts of Jesus, The Guide to Peace and Happiness*. It was a compilation of Roy's choice of the essential teachings of Jesus.

> These precepts separated from the mysterious dogmas and historical records, appear, on the contrary, to the compiler to contain not only the essence of all that is necessary to instruct mankind in their civil duties, but also the best and only means of obtaining forgiveness of sins, the favor of God and strength to overcome our passions and to keep his commandments.[3]

He omitted the historical narratives and references to the miraculous. The historical material, Roy felt, was subject to doubt and the miraculous unlikely to capture Hindu imagination. His selection, he hoped, would have the "desirable effect of improving the hearts and minds of men of different religious persuasions and degrees of understanding."[4] It is not certain what response Roy expected from his Christian missionary friends. Perhaps he anticipated support for his commendation of Jesus's teachings to Hindus, or an invitation to continuing dialogue. The response, in any case, was one of condemnation and hostility. At the heart of the Christian response to Roy was the accusation that he focused on the ethical teachings of Jesus to the exclusion of the central claim of these texts: that salvation is possible only through the atoning sacrifice of Jesus on the cross.

Swami Vivekananda

Swami Vivekananda (1863–1902), one of the most influential Hindu teachers in recent times and the first to teach in the west, made a special appeal for attentiveness to the teachings of Jesus. In his introduction to the Bengali translation of *The Imitation of Christ*, a work attributed to the medieval Catholic monk, Thomas Kempis (ca.1380–1471), Vivekananda cautioned his fellow Hindus not to belittle the text because the author is Christian. This medieval Christian work fascinated Vivekananda and it was the only text, along with the *Bhagavadgītā*, that he kept with him during his years of traveling around India after the death of his beloved teacher, Ramakrishna. He could understand and identify with the author of this work whose ideals and way of life closely resembled the aspirations and values of a traditional Hindu renunciant. Vivekananda admired the author's radical renunciation, his thirst for purity and his unceasing spiritual effort. Vivekananda likened *The Imitation of Christ* to the *Bhagavadgītā* in its spirit of complete self-surrender and saw the author as embodying the Hindu ideal of devotion to God as a servant to a master.[5]

Vivekananda narrated the story of Jesus for inspiration on the occasion when some of the disciples of his teacher, Sri Ramakrishna, took monastic vows. As described in one account, he told "the story of the Lord Jesus, beginning with the wonderous mystery of his birth through his death on to the resurrection. Through the eloquence of Narendra, the boys were admitted into that apostolic world wherein Paul has preached the gospel of the Arisen Christ and spread Christianity far and wide. Naren made his plea to them to become Christs themselves, to aid in the redemption of the world; to realize God and deny themselves as the Lord Jesus had done."[6] Years later, Gandhi, like Vivekananda, sought the heart of Christianity and found it in Jesus's Sermon on the Mount. These words, wrote Gandhi, "went straight to my heart."[7]

Roy, Vivekananda, Gandhi and others, we must note, were commending Jesus and his teachings in a historical context where Christianity was virtually inseparable from colonialism and in which missionaries denounced Hinduism as superstitious, idolatrous and polytheistic. They all labored to correct these stereotypes. The negative institutionalized Christian response to Hinduism, however, did not elicit a similar Hindu rejoinder to Jesus. All three interpreters were speaking from a Hindu perspective, in which commitment to a specific understanding of God did not rule out openness to and learning from other ways of understanding or, as Hindus say, other *darśanas* (ways of seeing). Hindus do not limit God's revelation and experience to Hindu sacred texts, places of worship and community. There is a deeply held Hindu insight that divine self-disclosure adapts itself to the diversity of human understanding. As Krishna states in the *Bhagavadgītā* (4:11), "the paths people take from every side are Mine (*mama vartmānuvartante manuṣyāh partha sarvaśāḥ*)."

Hindus have noted the similarity with Hinduism in the symbols and images, examples and parables used by Jesus in speaking about the religious life. They commend his freedom from greed, his transparent nonpossessiveness, and generous self-giving. Hindus have always understood renunciation of greed as a fundamental expression of the genuine religious life and the Hindu respect for Jesus does not surprise. Vivekananda advised his Christian listeners in the United States that they should be "ready to live in rags with Christ, than to live in palaces without him."[8] I venture to say that the Hindu response to Jesus is exceptional historically;

no central figure in one religion has been commended with such enthusiasm by seminal figures in another.

Acknowledging and Respecting Differences

The Hindu understanding and enthusiasm for Jesus as a teacher and exemplar of the religious life differ in significant ways from the mainstream Christian theological claims about Jesus's significance. Hindus must acknowledge and not reduce these differences to semantics. Christians are often frustrated by the scant regard among some Hindus for differences of doctrine. The famous *Ṛg Veda* text (I.164.46), "The One Being the wise speak of in many ways –*Ekam sad viprahāḥ bahudā vadanti,*" articulates an important Hindu teaching—that the oneness of God is not compromised by the many human ways of speaking. Its purpose is to help us know persons of other traditions, not as strangers with alien, false or rival deities, but as fellow beings whose God is our God. This powerful text, however, is used too often in interreligious dialogue to minimize the significance of differences within and among religions and to explain away these as entirely inconsequential or relegate differences to the non-essential aspects of religion.

Having said this, I must add also that a theocentric tradition like Hinduism, is too often cursorily dismissed by those advocating the necessity for faith in Jesus as an exclusive savior. Jesus is used to minimize the value of the understanding and experience of God in Hinduism. Jesus-centeredness is made the litmus test of religious authenticity. Representing Jesus in a manner that is dismissive of Hinduism, not only overlooks the unique Hindu embrace of Jesus, but makes it more difficult for us to be challenged and enriched by what his life and death teaches about the nature of God and the meaning of human existence. The face of Jesus will be identified with those who triumphantly denounce Hinduism in his name. This face will not be attractive or inviting.

The time has come for us to acknowledge our differences in understanding Jesus's identity, take note of distinctive Hindu Christologies, learn in humility from each other, and deepen the friendship that our mutual interest in Jesus and our appreciation of his significance make possible. Good relationships do not require sameness of vision or the abandonment of distinctive self-understanding. The beauty of a good relationship is often found in the creative encounter of difference. Our relationship, as Hindus and Christians, requires, like any good human relationship, attentive nurturing and nourishment. We must not be indifferent to or take our friendship for granted.

The Controversy Over Conversion

I want to turn now to one of the principal sources of contemporary tension and contention in Hindu-Christian relationships. This is the debate in India and elsewhere, centered on the issue of conversion and evangelization. On the Hindu side, we hear repeated calls for the enactment of laws to prohibit conversion from one religion to another and, in some cases, we have seen the implementation of legislation. In 2006, for example, the Rajasthan Assembly passed the Rajasthan Dharma Swantantraya Bill, stating that, "No person shall convert or attempt to convert directly or otherwise any person from one religion to another by the use of force, or by allurement or by any fraudulent means nor shall any person abet such conversion."[9] Although this Bill, and others like it, do not make the act of converting from one religion to another illegal, consensus on the meaning of terms like "force," "allurement," and "fraudulent," is problematic, if not nearly impossible. Many of the responses, on the Christian side, present the issue as one of religious freedom and argue for the liberty of religious choice and the right to convert. Like proverbial ships in the night, passing each other without engagement, these representative arguments seem to provide no common basis from which the issue of conversion may be satisfactorily addressed. Conversion is a prime example of a challenge that we can face together with hope.

Despising the Convert

Although conversion from one religion to another is a complex phenomenon and often inseparable from the socio-political realities of the local context, the despising of the convert is widespread. The reasons for the depth of hostility directed to the convert are many and include the convert's attitude to the religious community that is left behind, in the embrace of a new one. At a fundamental level, the convert disturbs and unsettles us and our discomfort finds expression in antipathy. The act of embracing a different religious tradition sharply challenges our settled assumptions about the adequacy of our religious worldview. Conversion disturbs by holding out the possibility that our answers are not the only ones or the only satisfactory ones. We see the act of conversion as one of primal rejection and, because our traditions so deeply define our identities, as one of disloyalty to us and to our community.

Our response is accusatory. We characterize the convert as a childlike and immature individual, who is incapable of exercising choice and judgment. We prefer to think that the convert does not cross religious boundaries because of any legitimate dissatisfaction with inherited tradition or anything of intrinsic worth in the other tradition. It is less challenging for us to think of conversion as the consequence of coercion or material inducement and not as suggesting anything problematic in our tradition or attractive in the other. Many of us who are hostile to the convert do so from positions of power and privilege within our tradition. Since we experience our religious tradition as good for us, we assume that it is similarly good for all who are born into it. Through circumstances of birth and opportunity, we live in our tradition without ever experiencing the oppression and violence that demeans and negates our dignity and self-worth. We do not see how what may be good for us may not be good for others, whose experiences within our faith may be quite different. It is instructive, for example, that the largest number of converts from the Hindu traditions in India to Buddhism, Christianity and Islam come from the so-called untouchable castes. Yet, Hindu responses to conversion rarely demonstrate any self-critical reflection on the significance of this fact.

On the other side of the picture, the convert is welcomed and celebrated in his adopted religion. The winning of converts is represented as confirmation of religious claims to superiority and justification of arguments for the false or incomplete teachings of other traditions. The convert is championed as the insider who reveals authoritatively the unworthiness of the religious tradition that one has abandoned. The convert is used as an "expert" witness in the case made against one's community and, in doing so, reinforces one's ostracism and alienation. The convert too often becomes a pawn in a power struggle between our traditions.

Sharing Our Traditions

Most of the religious traditions of our world share the conviction that their teachings and practices are beneficial to human beings. This conviction expresses itself in a desire and willingness to share these with others, even though traditions have adopted historically different methods for such dissemination of their teachings. Hindu traditions are not unfamiliar with the religious motive of sharing one's conviction and persuading others about its validity. To claim otherwise is not to be faithful to important strands of Hinduism. In the *Bhagavadgītā* (18: 68-69), for example, the teacher, Krishna, speaks of sharing his teachings with others as a priceless service (*na ca tasmān manuṣyeṣu kaścin me priyakṛttamaḥ*).

At the same time, the traditions of India evolved a certain ethos that guided the nature of their relationships. The absence of institutionalization and centralization meant that there were no systematic and sustained efforts to supplant different viewpoints. Discussions among the traditions were, on the whole, dialogical and could even result in conversion to the other's viewpoint. Persons with different religious commitments belonged to the same larger religio-cultural community, where boundaries were flexible and permeable. There was and is no negativistic notion regarding the fact of religious diversity. This is seen as a natural reflection of the diversity of human nature and experience. A widely shared understanding of the limits of human reason and symbols resulted in the understanding that truth always exceeded the comprehension and description of any one tradition, and justified relationships of theological humility.[10]

As we reflect on the historical entry of Christianity into this religious ethos, we must be cognizant of both the antiquity and diversity of Christianity. The Christian tradition in India has a long history. The Eastern Orthodox churches, for example, trace their arrival to the first century and have a history that is not connected with any colonial enterprise. We must also be careful not to causally equate colonialism and Christianity. Some of my Christian friends remind me that their encounter with the tradition was through fellow Indians, and not western missionaries. Yet it is also true that Christianity made an impact on Hinduism as a carriage in the train of western colonialism. It became associated, in reality, and in the minds of Hindus, with imperialism and with the arrogance and disdain the colonizer had for Hinduism. This association lingers and continues to inform and influence Hindu attitudes to Christianity. Imperialist political claims were seen as finding echo in exclusive theological claims to revelation and salvation. Christian theology, in relation to Hinduism, was and still remains significantly mission-oriented.

The identification, during the colonial period, between the Christianity and the culture of the west, resulted in the experience of these as inseparable. This identity between religion and culture, along with the fear that converts may revert to ancestral practices, led to systematic efforts to define a Christian identity over and against the prevailing Hindu ones. Christian converts took on new names from the Biblical texts, renamed villages to reflect their new faith, constructed churches following the architectural models of Europe, and adopted new musical forms. In many cases, converts also adopted new forms of dress and cuisine. Such forms of self-definition help a community, especially a minority one, to maintain its new identity.

At the same time, such deliberately sharp distinctions between self and other are a source of tension and resentment. This is especially so when the basis of such distinction is the claim also to religious superiority, and when the other (Hindu) is seen as fallen and in need of religious rescue. The nature of the Christian church as a voluntary association with membership implied and necessitated boundaries, and also a sharp distinction from Hindus. This significant dimension of identity was entirely absent from Hinduism and engendered also a sharp sense of difference between self and other. Colonialism, exclusive theology, identification with and adoption of missionary culture, and voluntary membership in a new religious community, separated the convert from the larger community and intensified fear, resentment and suspicion. It is important that Christians take seriously the legitimate Hindu concerns about conversion, and especially the suspicions about a Christian program for world religious conquest.

Although some of the long-established Christian churches in India have made theological and cultural efforts to address some of the tensions between our two traditions, the fruits of these efforts are not well-known among both Hindus and Christians. It is also true that many of the newer Christian missions are evangelical in orientation and aggressive towards Hinduism. The consequence is that Hindus continue to imagine and experience Christianity as an exclusive religion that is not open to the religious claims and experiences of others, and which is concerned primarily with increasing its institutional power and domination through conversion. Such perceptions induce uneasiness, resentment, and defensiveness.

We must admit the difficulty of building relationships when one assumes that, in the eyes of the other, one's convictions are false and without salvific value. Hindus have the perception that mission is the most important concern of Christianity and they are not generally aware of the internal theological diversity of the Christian tradition and the current debates about mission. They will be surprised to discover voices of support within Christianity, for their own struggles with proselytization.

The Necessity for Dialogue

Clearly, Hindus and Christians need to come together in dialogue on this divisive issue. Such dialogue will help us to discover areas of mutual agreement and clarify our concerns. We should agree immediately that religious faith is meaningful only when freely chosen. No tradition is served if converts are gained through unethical methods of coercion, through the promise of economic or political rewards, or through misrepresentation of oneself or other. Human vulnerability in times of material and emotional need must not be exploited for the purpose of gaining converts. Our traditions commend generosity as an end in itself, and as an outpouring of love and compassion that is free from the expectation of reward. The highest gifts in the Hindu tradition are those given for the sake of giving and without expectation of return (*dātavyam iti yad dānaṁ diyate 'nupakāriṇe*).[11]

Hindus must also recognize that conversion is not always the consequence of aggressive proselytization or inducement. Converts may be attracted to the worldview of another tradition. Some may be seeking an affirmation of their dignity and worth as human beings that they find promised and articulated in other traditions. The freedom to engage in religious inquiry and choice, honored in Hinduism, must not be compromised. The dependence of the state as the arbiter among religions in the matter of conversion is a sad concession of our own failure to find a mutually acceptable way forward. The empowerment of the state to intervene in matters of religious relationships will, I believe, work to the detriment of all religions.

Dialogue and Caste

Our dialogue of hope must include also a conversation on the caste system. There are many Christians who see the Hindu concern with conversion as a disguised effort to preserve the privileges and power relationships inherent in the caste system. Such a perception, like the equation of Christianity only with conversion, reflects a monolithic view of the Hindu tradition, and ignores the controversial nature of the caste structure in Hinduism and the continuing history of challenge to the system by reform-minded Hindus and movements. It ignores also the fact that even the Christian church in India has not been able to free itself from the social inequities and expressions of caste.

There is a theological vision at the heart of both Hinduism and Christianity that invalidates assumptions of inequality, impurity, and indignity that are at the foundations of caste belief and practice. This must be recognized and affirmed by both traditions. The foundation of this vision is the Hindu teaching that God exists equally in all beings (*samaṁ sarveṣu bhūteṣu tiṣṭantam parameśvaram*).[12] When the implications for human relationships are enunciated, they are done so in terms of equality. Hindu teachers throughout the ages, like Tiruvalluvar (2 BCE), Tirumular 6 CE), Basaveshwara (12 CE), Ramananda (15 CE), Kabir (16 CE), and Eknath (16 CE), were inspired by this vision and spoke of human unity and equality before God.

While some are able to escape the oppression of caste through conversion, greater good and change for many more may be achieved by the mutual support and transforming influence that the example of one religion may have on another. Such influence depends on developing a relationship of trust. Trust provides the secure ground on which we can stand, to be self-critical in the presence of people of our own and other traditions. It is the soil in which truth can flourish and where difficult questions that we want to ask of each other can be raised. It is our best hope for mutual understanding and transformation. Christians must understand the complexity of Hinduism and, in particular, the contested nature of caste and the chorus of voices, ancient and modern, protesting the practice of caste as a betrayal of Hinduism's highest teachings about human existence.

Conversion is a call to Hindus to investigate the relationship between theological teachings about human nature and structures of oppression. Hindus must be attentive to the voices of Dalit Christians and their experience of the tradition as oppressive. Conversion is also an opportunity for interreligious and intra-religious dialogue and action on a pervasive and persistent unjust social phenomenon that crosses religious boundaries.

Dialogue on the Meaning of Liberation

Hope and trust enable us to be challenged and enriched by each other's understanding of the meaning of liberation. Traditionally, the Hindu quest for liberation (*mokṣa*) occurred after a life of success in the world. The path to liberation is associated with renunciation and disinterest in the world. In those forms of Christianity, on the other hand, that emphasize the role of Jesus as a social prophet and his criticism of systems of domination, liberation is construed, not only as the overcoming of estrangement from God, but also as liberation from systems of domination and the creation of a just and inclusive social order. Activity directed to this end, such as the provision of education, healthcare, housing, food, and clothing are seen, from the Hindu viewpoint, as inducements to conversion and, by many Christians, as an expression of the meaning of their religious commitment. Hindus and Christians, however, agree on the necessity for working to overcome human suffering and this controversial matter offers us a wonderful opportunity for joining together in bringing relief to the poor and dispossessed, and in overcoming injustice. We both need a more comprehensive understanding of the sources of human suffering and of our roles in the midst of injustice and oppression.

Religion, Nationalism and Culture

I have highlighted some of the salient issues of concern that underline the necessity for continuing dialogue between our traditions. Some of these issues have greater significance in particular geographical locations.

Today, one of the very important historical developments in the Hindu tradition is the establishment of Hindu communities in various parts of our world. In these societies, Hindus wish to participate fully in the lives of their new homelands while preserving a distinctive religious identity. Although our interconnected world makes it difficult and even dangerous to ignore what happens elsewhere, we need also to ensure, as Hindus and Christians, that our relations in our own communities are not dictated and controlled by what transpires in India or elsewhere. Hindus need to be alert to the implications and dangers of popular movements and ideologies that narrowly equate the Hindu tradition with the nation-state or with a single culture. Ideologies of this kind undermine the ability of a tradition to make truth claims that are universal in nature and relevance. The status of Hindus as minorities in many parts of the world should sensitize them to the problems of defining national identity in ways that do not accommodate diverse religious and cultural identities. Hindus must be careful not to give uncritical support to any form of majority rule that does not accommodate diverse religious identities. The tradition is served best not only through support, but also by offering constructive criticism derived from distinctive Hindu experiences.

Looking to the Future with Hope

Hindus and Christians can look to the future and to our challenges with hope. Violence and animosity towards each other in the name of our respective traditions are rare events and can be averted by preventive measures at the local level. I referred earlier, to the historical friendship between our traditions. We must not overlook or take for granted the precious theological insights that we share and affirm, even as we do not overlook our differences. At the heart of these is our understanding that the meaning of our lives is inseparable from the belief that our universe has its source in the intentional creative act of an omniscient and loving being. The *Taittirīya Upaniṣad* (3.1.1) defines this being as, "That from which all have come, by which all are sustained and to which all return (*yato vā imāni bhūtāni jāyante yena jātāni jivanti yat prayanty-abhisaṁviśanti*)." We agree that in the light of God's infinite reality, our finite human theologies and symbols must be incomplete. *Taittīrya Upaniṣad* (2.9.1) reminds us again that God is the one "from which all words, along with the mind, turn back having failed to grasp (*yato vāco nivartante aprāpya manasā saha*)." A God whose nature and essence could be fully revealed in our words or who could be contained within the boundaries of our minds would not be the one proclaimed in our traditions. Our confession of the limits of our human understanding before God is a powerful justification for a relationship of humility, respect, mutual learning, and sharing. We share also a value for the dignity and equal worth of every human being derived from life having its source in God, who is both immanent and transcendent. The *Bhagavadgītā* (18:61) describes God as abiding in the hearts of all beings (*iśvaraḥ sarvabhūtānāṁ hṛddeśe 'rjuna tiṣṭati*). The value of the human being is derived from embodying God who has ultimate value. We agree that our knowledge of God is not meaningful unless it finds expression in a compassionate way of being. We profess and express our value and commitment to God by our love and value for all in which God entered and is present. Our reverence for life that has its origin in God is the source of our loyalty to non-injury (*ahiṁsā*) as a cardinal ethical principle.

This shared theological and ethical ethos is significant and must inspire our relationships, helping us to go beyond tolerance and towards active efforts at understanding. We need relationships that enable us to listen and to share, to ask questions and to be questioned. We need relationships that inspire cooperative action to overcome unjust and oppressive structures of all kinds and that work to heal and transform our communities through the practice of justice. In a world that yearns and longs for peace among religions, may Hindus and Christians, friends for centuries, lead the way.

References

1 This is a revised version of the 2008 Lambeth Interfaith Lecture that I delivered at the Lambeth Palace, London, U.K., at the invitation of the Archbishop of Canterbury, Dr. Rowan Williams.

2 Cited in Cromwell Crawford, *Ram Mohan Roy* (NY: Paragon House Publishers, 1987), 47.

3 Cited in M.M. Thomas, *The Acknowledged Christ of the Indian Renaissance* (Madras: Christian Literature Society, 1970),10.

4 Crawford, *Ram Mohan* Roy, 47.

5 CW 8: 159-61.

6 His Eastern and Western Disciples, *The Life of Swami Vivekananda,* 8th ed. (Calcutta: Advaita Ashrama, 1974), 159. Naren is the shortened version of his pre-monastic name, Narendra.

7 M. K. Gandhi, *An Autobiography* (Middlesex: Penguin Books, 1982), 77.

8 CW 8: 213.

9 "Anti-conversion bill passed in Rajasthan," https://wwrn.org/articles/21095/.

10 This is not to deny those historical moments when rivalries existed and even became violent. I am commenting here on a general disposition.

11 *Bhagavadgītā* 17:20.

12 *Bhagavadgītā* 13:28.

CHAPTER FIVE

DIVINE HOSPITALITY IN THE HINDU TEMPLE: RITUAL AND THE CROSSING OF RELIGIOUS BOUNDARIES

I commenced the discussion in chapter one with a description of the ritual installation of a *mūrti* at the Hindu Temple in Maple Grove, Minnesota, highlighting the nature of the *mūrti* as a living embodiment of the divine. The *mūrti* is viewed, not merely as a symbol of God as Viṣṇu, but as God's living embodiment in this world.[1] Viṣṇu is understood to have the city of Maple Grove as his abode.

This theological understanding of the nature of the *mūrti* is quite prominent in the tradition and community of Śrīvaiṣṇavas, who look to the religious poetry of the *ālvārs* (500–850 CE), centered on the love of Viṣṇu, as authoritative. The most influential and famous systematizer and exponent of the theology of Vaiṣṇavism is Rāmānuja (ca.12 CE), whose interpretation is referred to as Qualified Nondualism (Viśiṣṭādvaita) to distinguish it from the Nondual (Advaita) theology of Śaṅkara (ca. 8 CE). Although sharing with Śaṅkara the view that the infinite *brahman* is the only reality, Rāmānuja contends that *brahman* is internally complex and diverse. The all-inclusive *brahman* contains within itself a real diversity consisting of unconscious matter (*acit*) and conscious selves (*cit*). For Śaṅkara, on the other hand, *brahman* is the single ontological reality and all differences express the variety of forms and names but not ultimate being. In spite of such significant theological differences, Rāmānuja's theological understanding of the nature of the *mūrti* has exerted profound influence on Hindu tradition, and has been widely adopted even within the tradition of Śaṅkara and in those institutions that continue Śaṅkara's legacy.

There are also reformist Hindu traditions that reject the doctrine of the *mūrti* as a living embodiment of God. Prominent among these is the Arya Samaj, founded by Swami Dayananda Saraswati (1824–1883). Dayananda Saraswati equated the use of *mūrtis* with idolatry and viewed it as a symptom of the degeneration of the Hindu tradition from its pristine teachings in the Vedas. In Dayananda's words, "People never gain knowledge by the worship of material objects, on the contrary they forget even what they have previously acquired. Knowledge is increased by serving the learned and by associating with them - not by image worship."[2] Hindu temples affiliated with this group do not have altars with *mūrtis* for ceremonial worship. Rituals center on offerings into the sacred fire. Dayananda Saraswati also rejected the teaching of divine incarnation (*avatāra*) and affirmed the formless nature of God. There are other traditions in which *mūrtis* are used but are seen as symbols that are helpful for focusing the mind in meditation or prayer.[3]

My focus in this discussion, however, is with clarifying the orthodox Hindu understanding of the meaning of the *mūrti*, especially as articulated in the Vaiṣṇava tradition. This clarification is the necessary prelude for describing the nature of the Hindu temple and domestic worship and for considering the requirements of participation. Such analysis enables us to reflect on the implications for outsider participation in Hindu rituals.

Mūrti As the Living Embodiment of God

According to Rāmānuja, the *mūrti* or *arcā* embodiment of God is one of the five forms of divine manifestation.[4] In his supreme (*para*) form, God eternally abides in the heavenly world. The emanations (*vyūhas*) of God preside over the functions of creation, preservation, and destruction. At periodic intervals, God incarnates, and persons such as Rama and Krishna are believed to be earthly incarnations (*avatāras/vibhavas*) of God. God resides in the heart of all beings as the inner controller (*antaryāmin*). Finally, and most importantly for Vaiṣṇavas, is the presence of God in the icon (*arcāvatāra*). This form is wholly God, and is not understood as contradicting the all-pervasive presence of God in the universe. This view of the *mūrti* must be distinguished from perceptions of *mūrtis* as just useful forms for focusing the mind during periods of worship or meditation, or as visual theologies that symbolically communicate insights about the nature of God. *Mūrtis* may certainly facilitate concentration at the time of worship and serve didactic purposes, but these are secondary purposes for the devout Hindu. The understanding of the *mūrti* as a living incarnation (*avatāra*) is a radically different theological claim. It is this understanding that makes worshipful interaction (*pūja*), especially in the temple, possible and meaningful. It also explains the faith, expressed in chapter one, that God resides in the temple in a form that is real and tangible.

Transformation from Object to Living Embodiment

How does an object become a living embodiment of God, a proper recipient of ritual worship in the Hindu temple? Every step in the making of a *mūrti* for ritual worship is governed by ritual prescriptions and guidelines. As Diana Eck notes, traditional texts (*śilpaśāstras*) "specify the proper proportion of the parts of the body, the appropriate number of arms, the gestures of the hands (*mudrās*), the emblems and weapons to be held in the hands, and the appropriate animal mount (*vāhana*)."[5] Religious artists (*śilpins*) closely follow these instructions. There are ritual instructions even for the selection of the material to be used.[6]

Once the *mūrti* is prayerfully and properly fashioned, it undergoes a series of consecratory rituals, culminating in what is referred to as *prāṇapratiṣṭhā*, or the establishment of the breath of life in the *mūrti* (*prāṇa*, life breath; *pratiṣṭhā,* establishment). The final step in this elaborate ritual occurs when the artist completes his work by opening the eyes of the *mūrti*. One of the prayers (*mantras)* during the ceremony articulates well the worshipper's awareness of the paradox, mystery and grace of inviting God to be present in the *mūrti*.

> Lord, you are omnipresent, yet I am inviting you to be present in this form as one would use a fan to the air. Just as the divine fire, *lying hidden in the wood comes out to be experienced and savored,* let your presence be felt by your devotees.[7]

The point of both analogies in this verse is the same. God, who is present everywhere and pervades everything, like the air or like heat in a piece of wood, graciously becomes manifest and receives worship in response to the devotee's longing. The divinity present in every object becomes manifest in a particular object through a ritual of invocation.

The consecrated *mūrti* is housed in the innermost shrine of the temple, referred to, in Sanskrit, as the *garbhagṛha*, that is the "womb room." Located at the center of the temple, the womb room is identified externally by the tallest (*śikhara*) of a series of pyramidal or peak-like spires rising progressively from the entrance of the temple. The *śikhara* denotes honor and eminence. The womb room is usually a dimly lit, cube-shaped enclosure, with minimal decoration, regarded as the dwelling place of God.[8] In many of the temples in the United States, established by Hindu immigrants from the Caribbean, the space housing the *mūrti* is not so dramatic. Many of these are homes or other purpose buildings converted into temples. The *mūrtis* are kept in an open area, accessible to all. In some of the newer temples constructed in North America, devotees are able to approach the *mūrtis* directly. The Vishnu Mandir and the Devi Mandir in Toronto, Canada, for example, have open altars that enable worshippers to have direct access to the *mūrtis*. This is a deviation from the tradition that only the priests have the requisite purity to interact directly with the *mūrti*. This is not true, however, of all North American temples.[9] In the orthodox temple, the priest (*pūjārī*) or priests serving and caring for the *mūrti* are alone permitted to enter the innermost shrine.

Pūja: Hospitality and Honor to God

Once the *mūrti* is properly consecrated and is a living embodiment of God, the temple becomes a special dwelling place of God. It is now a sacred environment where everything is centered and focused on God, who is honored through a series of hospitality offerings (*upacāras*) spoken of generally as *pūjā*. These are about sixteen in number and include the invitation to receive worship (*āvāhana*), the invitation to a seat (*āsana*), the washing of the feet (*pādya*), and acts of adoration through the offering of flowers (*puṣpa*), the burning of incense (*dhūpa*), the waving of lights (*dīpa*), and food (*naivedya*). Worship always concludes with the offering of *prasāda*, that is food, which has been ritually offered to God.

The *mūrti* in the Hindu temple is regarded as the king of kings (or the queen of queens in the case of a feminine form of God). Although regional traditions in India differ, worship generally starts in the quiet dawn when the deity is roused from sleep with soft, solemn music and the recitation of sacred verses. The awakening ceremony is followed by the ceremonial bath, after which the deity is anointed with sandal paste, dressed in royal robes, and decked with ornaments and flowers. These ceremonies are usually done with the *mūrti* screened from public viewing, since such viewing would be considered inappropriate and intrusive. The public is invited to see God only after these rituals are completed and the *mūrti* is properly adorned. Hymns (*stuti*) are sung and offerings are made at regular intervals during the day. Worship ends with an elaborate evening light (*āratī*) offering, after which the deity enjoys a nightly rest.

In explaining the meaning of such worship, Diana Eck cites appropriately the well-known Vaiṣṇava theologian, Pillai Lokācārya, who speaks of God entrusting God-self to the care of human devotees.

> This is the greatest grace of the Lord, that being free He becomes bound, being independent He becomes dependent for all His service on his devotee. In other forms the man belonged to God but behold the supreme sacrifice of Īśvara, here the Almighty becomes the property of the devotee. He carries Him about, fans Him, plays with Him-yea, the Infinite has become finite, that the child soul may actually grasp, understand and love Him.[10]

The priest caring for the *mūrti* and the worshipper reverently observing the ritual share a profound sense that God is the immediate recipient of this loving honor and hospitality.

As we noted in chapter one, the presence of a consecrated *mūrti* transforms the family home into an abode of God and most Hindu homes have a room or a corner of a room set aside for the purpose of *pūja*. Great care is taken to maintain its purity and sanctity. Here is kept the *mūrti* of the family's chosen form of God (*iṣṭadevata*). The *mūrti* is a potent reminder of God's presence and the home becomes a sacred space in which all aspects of life are centered on God. In the *mūrti*-form, God is the beloved household guest around whom all activities revolve and to whom everything is dedicated. Daily worship in the Hindu home is not as elaborate as in the temple and consists usually of selected *pūja* procedures. Common is the offering of light (*āratī*), waved in a clockwise direction before the *mūrti* and then passed on to family members, who receive the blessings of God by placing their hands near the flame and touching their eyes and forehead. Food, a portion of which may be offered first to God, is distributed, and sandalwood paste is applied to the forehead of family members present.

Darśana (Seeing God) and *Prasāda* (Receiving Blessings)

Although included in the *pūja* ritual, it is revealing to highlight and elaborate further on two elements that are especially important for participation in Hindu rituals. These are *darśana* and *prasāda*. We begin with *darśana*.

Darśana is a central practice of Hindu worship. We do not usually speak of visiting a Hindu temple for the purpose of worship, but we do speak often of going for *darśana*. The same term is employed often to describe the purpose for visiting a saintly person, a religious teacher (*guru*), or a site of pilgrimage such as a sacred river, mountain, or even a holy city.

There is no easy English equivalent for translating *darśana*. Eck speaks of it as "auspicious sight."[11] *Darśana* comes from the Sanskrit root "*dṛs*," meaning "to see." Although literally meaning "sight," it is not employed to describe all acts of seeing. It is reserved for describing the seeing of that which is imbued with religious meaning and may be rendered as "sacred seeing." It is most commonly used to describe the seeing of the *mūrti* in the Hindu temple. Hindus visit temples to stand before and look at the consecrated *mūrti*, fixed in the consciousness of seeing and standing in God's presence. The theology of the *arcāvatāra* or *mūrti*-embodiment of God makes *darśana* possible and meaningful. God graciously makes God-self accessible and available for the devotee's seeing and this act alone satisfies, for many Hindus, the purpose of visiting a temple. It is an intimate and immediate experience of God.

For the devout Hindu, *darśana* is a dual mode of experience. It is a profound sense of seeing God and, at the same time, a consciousness of being "seen" by God or standing in God's presence. In *darśana*, I see and know that I am seen. I am aware that God's eyes are upon me. To enhance this experience, the eyes of the *mūrti* are usually prominent and conspicuous and, as noted above, the final act in the ritual installation of a *mūrti* involves the opening of the eyes. An icon with eyes closed does not engender the sense of being seen by God. *Darśana* is a special communion between the devotee and God. To know that the eyes of God are upon me is to overcome feelings of anonymity and insignificance. Much of what transpires when Hindus visit temples and stand before a *mūrti* becomes inaccessible to the outsider, without an understanding of the experience of *darśana*.

The second prominent element of Hindu worship is *prasāda*. *Prāsada* is derived from the Sanskrit root "*prasad*," meaning "to be satisfied, pleased or happy." As a noun, *prasāda* refers to a gift or favor, especially one that is received from God. It is a gift that fills with joy. In the specific context of Hindu worship, *prasāda* describes that which is given to the worshipper at the end of worship and received as a special gift of God. Although *prasāda* is usually something edible such as a fruit, sugar crystals or even a complete meal, it may be a flower or even drops of water. The distinctive feature of *prasāda* is that the gift is received as coming from God. One of the hospitality acts in the performance of *pūja* in the temple or Hindu home, is the offering of food (*naivedya*). Some of this is distributed at the end of worship as *prasāda*. Hindu devotees visiting a temple usually take an edible offering, which the priest places before the *mūrti* on behalf of the worshipper. After God receives it, a portion of it is returned to the worshipper as *prasāda*. The manner in which an ordinary edible item gets transformed into *prasāda* is a revealing insight into Hindu worship and the significance of the *mūrti* as an embodiment of God.

Let us imagine that before visiting my favorite temple, I stop by a vendor on the road leading to the temple to select a few bananas for purchase. I pay the vendor, place the bananas in my bag and continue my journey to the temple. During this process, I do not think of the bananas as being different from the rows of bananas on the vendor's cart. After arriving at the temple, I make my way to the sanctum with my bananas, give these to the priest, and wait patiently as he takes my bananas to the *mūrti* and offers them with appropriate *mantras.* When he returns the bananas to me, a profound transformation occurs in my perception of the fruit. I immediately lift these to my head with reverence and joy. I receive the bananas with a heart full of gratitude. These are now no longer ordinary bananas from a vendor's cart, but *prasāda,* and there is a world of difference between the two. In fact, I will no longer use the word "bananas" to describe the fruits but speak of these only as *prasāda.*

It is evident that the bananas have not changed; they are not different in appearance and content. When, however, I receive the banana after the temple priest offers it to the *mūrti*, the living embodiment of God, I see it as *prasāda*, as a gift and blessing from God. This understanding brings about a corresponding change in my state of mind that may be best described as one of cheerful serenity and joy. *Prasāda* refers both to the tangible object received as the gift of God as well as the state of mind which this gift awakens.

An object becomes *prasāda* when it is seen as coming from God and when that perception results in a mental and emotional state of joyful gratitude. The value of the banana can no longer be measured by its purchase price. It has now become priceless. The worth of the gift comes from the gift-giver, who, in this case, happens to be God. If I offer this banana to a friend or family member, after my return from the temple, with the explanation that it is *prasāda*, the response will be one of joyful reverence and acceptance. *Prasāda* reminds us of God's generosity and loving grace. One never refuses *prasāda* and it is sacrilegious, in Hinduism, to offer *prasāda* for sale or to commercialize it in any way. It is only to be shared.

The Outsider and the Hindu Temple

With rare exceptions, there are no restrictions on non-Hindus entering Hindu temples. One exception is the temple of Jagannath (Lord of the Universe) in Puri, Orissa, where a sign on the temple gate announces, "Only Orthodox Hindus are allowed."[12] The reasons for the prohibition are not clear. Some speculate that it may be connected with attacks on the temple during the Mughal rule. The King of Puri, Gajapati King Dibya

Singha Deb, offered the explanation that since Puri is the original seat of the Lord, there is restriction on the entry of non-Hindus. However, they can have *darśana* of the Lord in other Jagannath temples elsewhere.[13] Stephen Huyler speculates that the reason is connected with the Hindu understanding of the doctrine of *karma,* and the belief that negative mental states generate undesirable outcomes.

> Those not trained in the customs of approaching and honoring a sacred image might consciously or unconsciously pollute it. In the same way that the power of images and sacred spaces is believed to be enhanced by prayers and positive actions, it may also be damaged by careless or malevolent gestures, thoughts, or actions.[14]

Quite recently, in a most interesting decision, the Tirumala Tirupati Devasthanamas, the group managing India's richest and perhaps most famous temple, the Tirupati Temple in Andhra Pradesh, prohibited the entry of all non-Hindus into the temple unless they signed a register affirming their faith in the deity, Lord Venkateshwara.[15] The signing of the register was a voluntary act in the past and the recent enforcement was triggered by the refusal of a devout Christian political leader to comply. The temple body is concerned also about Christian proselytization in the precincts of the temple.

It will be very helpful if temples like the Jagannath in Puri, Orissa, and the Tirupati in Andhra Pradesh clarified their reasons for excluding non-Hindus. Who, for example, is an orthodox Hindu? What does it mean to have faith in Lord Venkateshwara? Such theological clarification will help us to understand how these temples conceive of Hindu worship and the corresponding requirements for participation.

Barring these prominent exceptions, most Hindu temples warmly welcome guests of other faiths, providing that the visitors observe temple norms. These include the removal of shoes before entering the worship space and modesty in dress. All temples have designated areas for the storage of shoes. Visitors should also avoid pointing their feet towards the *mūrti* if they choose to sit on the floor.

The Hindu temple, as described above, is a sacred space where God makes God-self accessible and present in a special *mūrti* form. A temple is referred to as a *devālaya* (*deva,* God; *ālaya,* house) or abode of God. One enters a Hindu temple as God's guest and the Hindu priest (*pūjāri*), the servant of God, happily welcomes the guest with a hospitality that is ancient and deep-rooted, both cultural and religious. The practice of a non-Hindu going to a Hindu temple as an observer who does not wish to participate in rituals is a relatively recent one. It is now quite common in Hindu temples in North America, where non-Hindu members of the community and students from colleges and high schools visit regularly to learn about Hindu practices. There are also many visitors from Christian churches, learning about their neighbors of other faiths.

Divine Hospitality to the Outsider

Most Hindu temple priests assume that the visitor has come to see God (*darśana*) and to receive the blessings (*prasāda*) of God. This assumption is easier since Hindu traditions are decentralized and do not require membership for participation. There is no tradition in Hindu temples, comparable to the non-sharing practice of communion in Catholic churches, of excluding non-Hindus from ritual participation. The Hindu priest expresses the hospitality of God and his own hospitality in a gracious and spontaneous inclusion of the visitor in the temple worship, assuming that the non-Hindu will be happy to be included. If the non-Hindu visitor happens to be present at the shrine during worship (*pūja* or *arcana*), they will be offered the same expressions of welcome and blessing as the Hindu visitor. These generally include *tilaka*, *āratī*. *caraṇāmṛta*, *sātari* and *prasāda*. *Tilaka* is sandal paste, vermillion or ash applied to the forehead as a mark of welcome and blessing. *Āratī* is the flame that is waved in a clockwise direction before the *mūrti* and then brought to the worshippers. A devout Hindu will lift one's hands towards the flame and then over one's head and face. *Caraṇāmṛta* is the water used to wash the feet of the *mūrti*. The priest gives drops of this to the worshippers for sipping. The *sātari* is a gold or silver crown, with the imprint of the *mūrti's* feet. It is placed on the head of the worshipper as a mark of blessing. Bowing one's head at the feet of God or a religious teacher (*guru*) is an expression of respect and humility. *Prasāda* is offering brought to the temple, usually edible, that is then distributed to the worshipper. All of these offerings to the worshipper by the Hindu priest reinforce the understanding of the *mūrti* as a living embodiment of God interacting with the visitor. Non-Hindus who wish to participate in Hindu temple rituals should not be fearful that errors may cause offence. Hindu priests understand well their lack of familiarity and give more value to intent and attitude than ritual correctness.

The Hindu temple priest feels a deep obligation to include the non-Hindu visitor in his ritual routines since he is God's agent, and God's hospitality and blessings are available to all who come to the temple. The choice is not on the part of the priest; it is with the visitor who must decide to accept or decline. No Hindu priest, however, will insist on the ritual participation of the non-Hindu visitor to the temple. A respectful gesture of declining (bringing the palms together and a bow of the head) will suffice, and the priest will move on to the next person. Hindus should see that such a gesture of decline may be born from a deep respect for the tradition and that its special theological claims that are not treated lightly.

Idolatry, Polytheism and Hindu Worship

The reluctance to participate in Hindu temple worship on the part of some Jews, Christians and Muslims is sometimes caused by concerns and fears about idolatry. Many from these religions equate *mūrti* with "idol" and condemn Hindu traditions as being idolatrous. The choice about participating in Hindu rituals is one that must be exercised on the basis of one's own theological commitments and one's understanding of the meaning of these in relation to the teachings and practices of other religions. It is important, however, that our understanding is true and faithful to the other's self-understanding. The clarifications that I offer here are not for the purpose of persuading others to participate in Hindu worship. I do so only to enhance interreligious understanding. At the same time, I believe that participation in the rituals of another tradition should be done with clarity about the theological and other assumptions underlying these.

If idolatry is construed as a simplistic equation of the uncreated and infinite God with a created and finite object, this is certainly not the understanding of the Hindu worshipper standing before a *mūrti*. Hindu theological traditions, dualistic and nondualistic, exemplify an appreciation of God as both immanent and transcendent, near and far, beyond name and form and with name and form. The language of paradox, as in this verse from the *Īśa Upaniṣad* (5), is familiar to Hindus when speaking of God:

> It moves, it does not move;
> It is far and near likewise.
> It is inside all of this:
> It is outside all of this.

Hindu texts, like the *Bhagavadgītā*, invite us continuously to see God as present in every form and to see every form as existing in God.

> I am the taste in water, the brilliance in the moon and sun, the sacred syllable (Om) in all the Vedas, the sound in air and virility in men.
>
> I am the pure fragrance in the earth, the radiance in fire, life in all beings and austerity in ascetics (7:8-9).

This vision, as the verse above makes clear, in not an anthropomorphic one. Hindus journey from afar for *darśana* of the Himalayan peaks and the rushing waters of the River Ganges. Nature is a vast theater in which the divine is known and experienced. Reflecting on her Christian fears about worshipping nature and not God, and on looking only to history as the medium for God's revelation, Diana Eck invites us to enlarge our understanding of these as opposites.

> But "nature" and "history" are not true opposites. Do we really need to choose one and not the other? Both nature and history are revelatory. Both are infused with the energy and breath of God. If I can attest to the life of the Spirit in the daring history of the modern Christian ecumenical movement, I can also insist upon the presence of the Spirit in the cyclical renewal of nature.[16]

The general Hindu theological orientation is to see the omnipresent God as present in and pervading the universe and all forms within it, and also beyond it. God is not limited to any particular form. A traditional Hindu prayer for forgiveness movingly expresses the Hindu sense of the paradox of all worship:

> In my meditations, I have attributed forms to You who transcend all forms.
> In my songs of praise, I have contradicted that you are indescribable.
> In my pilgrimage, I have denied your omnipresence.
> O Lord of the universe, forgive me these limitations.[17]

The nature of Hindu worship and the issue of idolatry was one of the topics of discussion at a historic Hindu-Jewish Leadership Summit Meeting in Jerusalem (February 17–20, 2008).[18] Perhaps the most significant affirmation of the joint declaration reads as follows:

> It is recognized that the One Supreme Being, both in its formless and manifest aspects, has been worshipped by Hindus over the millennia. This does not mean that Hindus worship "gods" and "idols". The Hindu relates to only the One Supreme Being when he/she prays to a particular manifestation.

This does not imply that Jews will or should now feel comfortable about participating in Hindu worship, but it certainly marks a significant step in Jewish understanding of the theology of the *mūrti* and its use in Hindu worship.

Another issue of concern about Hindu worship for Jews, Christians and Muslims, members of what is now commonly referred to as the Abrahamic religions, is the multiplicity of images and names for the divine in the Hindu tradition. This phenomenon is widely regarded as polytheistic and denounced. Most Hindu temples, while having a central *mūrti*, will have also many other forms of God. In "monotheistic consciousness," according to Diana Eck, "this singular is the proper number for questions of Truth: There is one God, one Only-Begotten Son of the Father, one Seal of the Prophets, One Holy Book, one Holy Catholic and Apostolic Church."[19]

Here again, it is important for people of other faiths to engage the Hindu understanding of the oneness and many-ness of God. Although it is true that the many-ness of the forms in which God is represented in the Hindu tradition reflects the religious and cultural diversity of the Indian sub-continent, each region having its own favorite representation of God, there is ancient theological interpretation of this diversity that is pervasive. This understanding is expressed earliest in a famous *Ṛg Veda* hymn (I. 164. 45-46).[20]

> Speech hath been measured out in four divisions.
> The Wise who have understanding know them.
> Three kept in close concealment cause no motion;
> of speech men only speak the fourth division (45).
> They call him Indra, Mitra, Varuna, Agni, and he is
> the noble-winged Garutman.
> The One Being, the wise call by many names:
> they call it Agni, Yama, Matarisvan (46).

Verse I.164.45 provides the context with an insight about the nature of human speech. It does so by presenting the totality of speech as consisting of four quarters. Human speech comprises only a quarter of the total speech potential. In describing the three-quarters of speech as "kept in close concealment" and causing "no motion," the verse suggests powerfully the language of silence and the ultimate inexpressibility of the One Being (*ekam sat*) referred to in the verse following.

Hindu sacred texts and tradition remind us constantly that, in relation to God, our language is always limited and inadequate. God is always more than we can define, describe or understand with our finite minds and fragmented language. No representation of the divine in image or words can ever be complete. When we employ our limited language, a fraction of the total potentiality of language, to speak of the limitless One, our language will be diverse. We use many names (Indra, Mitra, Varuna, Agni, Yama, Matarisvan, Garutman) not because the gods are many, but because of the limits of human language and experience. The different names are not just names. Each name also points to a different way of imagining and understanding the nature of the One Being and each name and way of understanding implies its own peculiar limitation.

Acknowledging the diversity of human names and ways of understanding God, the *Ṛg Veda* text is unambiguous in its assertion that God is one (*ekam*). It is the one God that is called and imagined differently. Those who name and worship God as Indra, Agni or Varuna are not, in reality, addressing themselves to different beings but to the one true being. One name alone is not true and all others false, and one name does not include or represent all others. Each is a name for the One. The text rejects the existence of many gods and proclaims the truth of the One. As *Maitrī Upaniṣad* (5:1) states this teaching:

> You are Brahma, you are Vishnu too;
> You are Rudra, you are Prajapati.
> You are Agni, Varuna, Vayu:
> You are Indra, you are the Moon.

Hindus usually think about God in other traditions through the lens of this verse. Extended to other traditions, we may say that the text does not allow for a Jewish, Christian, Muslim or Hindu God. It does recognize multiple understandings, while denying multiple divinities. The oneness of God is not compromised by the many-ness of names and forms or ways of speaking. This insight enables us to think of persons in other traditions, not as strangers with alien, false or rival deities, but as fellow beings whose God is our God. This outlook explains the ease with which some Hindus enter other places of worship and participate in alien rituals.

It is important for me to emphasize that the Hindu understanding of divine many-ness and oneness is not a theologically elitist position. It is one that is broadly shared by Hindus. Of course, given the diversity of Hindu traditions and the vast number of practitioners, one will surely find some who regard deities as separate realities. I venture to say, however, that these are fewer in numbers.

Theology and Crossing Religious Boundaries

The Christian theologian, Thomas Thangaraj noted and reflected on crossing religious boundaries while observing the ease with which his Hindu friend, Ganga, a visiting scholar at an American University, "attended a nearby Methodist church every Sunday, participating in all the elements of the liturgy, including the Eucharist."[21] Upon inquiry, Ganga explained that in the absence of Hindu temples, the Methodist church was a sacred space where he could worship God. Ganga was undoubtedly expressing the perspective of the *Ṛg Veda* text above. Thangaraj contrasted his own religious inhibitions with Ganga's freedom.

> How can my Hindu friend worship God easily in a Christian setting, while I have so much difficulty doing the same in a Hindu temple? When I consider this problem carefully, it becomes clear that the ideas and practices that shaped my religious devotion are very different from those that shape Ganga's. My religious experience has produced an approach to other traditions that makes it difficult for me to pray with my Hindu friend and in a Hindu setting of worship.[22]

Although there are Hindus who problematically minimize religious difference on the basis of this *Ṛg Veda* text, the text itself does not suggest this. Instead of underplaying differences, we may infer from the text the necessity for attentiveness to diverse ways of speaking about God. It is the wise, after all, who speak differently. Theological diversity is not dismissed here as the consequence of ignorance. By attributing differences to the speech of the wise, the text invites a respectful and inquiring response to religious diversity. We must not hastily and arrogantly denounce the sacred speech of the other as undeserving of sincere and serious contemplation.

The value of this text is to be found particularly in the articulation of an overlooked implication of God's oneness—the fact that my neighbor of another faith, who speaks a different religious language, and I are addressing and relating ourselves to the same God. Through differences of names, symbols, cultures and theologies, we comfortably clothe God with an identity that is similar to our own and fail to recognize the one God in other theological and symbolic dresses. Discerning the truth of the "One Being the wise call by many names" is profoundly transformative. It explains, in part, the ease of Ganga, the Hindu, in crossing physical and theological boundaries and discovering God in a Methodist Church. The Hindu-Jewish declaration, discussed earlier, speaks of Hindus as relating to the "One Supreme Being."

The Hindu tradition, with rare exceptions, has not developed conversion ceremonies for those who wish to become Hindus.[23] This makes it easier for people of other traditions to participate in Hindu worship if they desire to do so. Hindus will not generally see it as problematic for a Christian, for example, to remain Christian while practicing Hindu rituals. This is also possible because Hindu temple worship is not usually congregational in structure and offers a great measure of freedom to the worshipper. The choice, however, is always with the worshipper to accept or reject the hospitality of God offered in the Hindu temple.

References

1 For a summary of both interpretations, see S. Chatterjee and D. Datta, *An Introduction to Indian Philosophy* (Kolkata: Calcutta University Press, 2008), 365-430.

2 Swami Dayananda Saraswati, *Light of Truth*, trans. Chiranjiva Bharadwaja (Delhi: Sarvadeshik Arya Pratinidhi Sabha, 1975), 378-379.

3 See J. T .F. Jordens, *Dayananda Sarasvati: His Life and Ideas* (Delhi: Oxford University Press, 1978).

4 See Vasudha Narayanan, "Arcāvātara: On Earth as He is in Heaven," in *Gods of Flesh/Gods of Stone: Embodiment of Divinity in India,* eds. Joanne Punzo Waghorne, Norman Cutler, et al (Chambersburg: Anima Publications,1985), 54. For a more detailed discussion, see also J. N. Banerjea, *The Development of Hindu Iconography* (Delhi: Munshiram Manoharlal, 1974).

5 Diana Eck, *Darśan: Seeing the Divine Image in India* (Chambersburg: Anima Books, 1981), 51.

6 For a description of *mūrti*–making at the Puri-Jagannath temple in Orissa, see James J. Preston, "Creation of the Sacred Image: Apotheosis and Destruction in Hinduism" in *Gods of Flesh/Gods of Stone*, 9-32.

7 Quoted in commemorative magazine published (2006) to celebrate opening of the Hindu Temple, Maple Grove, Minnesota.

8 See Alain Danielou, *The Hindu Temple*, trans. Ken Henry (Rochester, Vermont: Inner Traditions, 2001).

9 It is revealing that Hindu immigrants from the Caribbean, especially from Guyana, Trinidad and Tobago, founded both of these Toronto temples. These communities have existed in the western world for over 160 years and reflect a process of change, adaptation and transformation of tradition. See Anantanand Rambachan, "Global Hinduism: The Hindu Diaspora," in *Contemporary Hinduism*, ed. Robin Rinehart (Santa Barbara: ABC-CLIO Inc., 2004),381-414.

10 Cited in Eck, *Darśan: Seeing the Divine Image in India*, 46.

11 Eck, *Darśan: Seeing the Divine Image in India*, 4.

12 https://www.ndtv.com/bhubaneshwar-news/controversies-over-jagannath-temples-entry-rules-495314.

13 "Non-Hindus can enter Jagannath Temples, except Shrine at Puri," http://www.thehindu.com/news/national/other-states/nonhindus-can-enter-jagannath-temples-except-shrine-at-puri/article2764219.ece

14 Stephen Huyler, *Meeting God: Elements of Hindu Devotion* (New Haven: Yale University Press, 1999), 255.

15 "Non-Hindus to sign Faith Forms to enter Tirumala Temple in Andhra Pradesh," http://indiatoday.intoday.in/story/non-hindus-to-sign-faith-form-to-enter-tirumala-temple-in-andhra-pradesh/1/210621.html.

16 Eck, *Encountering God*, 141.

17 Traditional prayer of unknown authorship. Cited in Anantanand Rambachan, *The Hindu Vision* (Delhi: Motilal Banarsidass, 1992), 7.

18 For a full declaration, see http://www.hafsite.org/pdf/2nd%20Jewish-Hindu%20Summit%20Final%20Declaration%2002-27-08.pdf.

19 Eck, *Encountering God*, 59.

20 Scholars regard the *Ṛg Veda* as the earliest of the Vedic texts (ca. 1500 BCE or earlier).

21 Thomas Thangaraj, *Relating to People of Other Religions* (Nashville: Abingdon Press,1997), 8.

22 Thangaraj, *Relating to People of Other Religions.*

23 The reformist Arya Samaj movement is one exception and has a purification (*shuddhi*) ceremony.

CHAPTER SIX

"WHO DO PEOPLE SAY I AM?": A HINDU CHRISTOLOGY[1]

Swami Vivekananda (1863-1902) is arguably the most influential interpreter of the Hindu tradition in recent times to both India and the west. In his eloquent speeches to the World Parliament of Religions (1893) and across the United States of America after the Parliament, Vivekananda both informed about and defined the Hindu tradition. Although Vivekananda identified himself most closely with the worldview of the Advaita Vedānta tradition, he sought to comprehensively define the essential elements of the Hindu tradition and to offer an interpretation of the relationship obtaining among its different streams. His imprint on the understanding of the Hindu tradition by Hindus and others remains indelible.

After Hinduism, the tradition that engaged Swami Vivekananda's attention and thought most significantly, was Christianity. There are many reasons for this. Swami Vivekananda inherited the history of the Brahmo Samaj's interest in Christ and Christianity. The Brahmo Samaj founder, Ram Mohan Roy (1774-1833) and his successor, Keshub Chandra Sen (1838-1884) spoke and wrote a great deal about Christianity. As a young man, Swami Vivekananda was active in the circles of the Brahmo Samaj and especially in the New Dispensation founded by Keshub Chandra Sen. He "attended meetings, lived among Brahmo students and loved to sing Brahmo songs."[2] Vivekananda was educated at the Scottish Church College in Calcutta, an institution founded by the Christian missionary, Alexander Duff. One assumes that he would have had significant exposure to Christianity and even read Christian texts. Christian missionaries were active in Calcutta and often ignited controversies. The ruling British elite identified closely with Christianity, which was de facto the religion of the state, and the alliance was obvious in the eyes of Hindu subjects. This chapter will focus on Vivekananda's Christology, understood as the theological discipline that offers a systematic reflection on the nature and significance of Jesus.

Vivekananda's Preface to *The Imitation of Christ*

Vivekananda's earliest known views about Christ and Christianity were expressed in a preface that he wrote to his Bengali translation of *The Imitation of Christ* (CW 8:159–161), a work attributed to the medieval Catholic monk, Thomas Kempis (ca. 1380-1471).[3] He translated six chapters of this work, added appropriate quotations from Hindu texts, and contributed these to a Bengali monthly journal. *The Imitation of Christ* engaged Vivekananda's attention in a special way, and it was the only text, other than the *Bhagavadgītā*, that he kept with him during his years of travelling around India after the death of his revered teacher, Sri Ramakrishna. Vivekananda translated and published *The Imitation of Christ* in order to present to Hindus what he understood to be the true spirit of Christianity. This spirit, Vivekananda felt, was absent from the lives of most Christians who Hindus encountered in day-to-day situations. Missionaries, according to Vivekananda, spoke of the ideal of renunciation, but this was never embodied in their lives.

In seeking to win legitimacy for the text among Hindus, Vivekananda was aware of the need to overcome antagonism towards Christianity, generated by missionary denunciation of Hinduism and aggressive proselytization. The catholicity of his viewpoint is reflected in the manner in which he employs the views of *Vaiśeṣika*, one of the orthodox schools of Indian philosophy, to make his argument. His point was that religious wisdom is not limited to teachings given by persons born in India. He was making a case for openness to the teachings of the text despite its foreign origin.

> To those of my countrymen, who under the influence of blind bigotry may seek to belittle this book because it is the work of a Christian, I shall quote only one aphorism of *Vaisheshika Darshana* and say nothing more. The aphorism is this: *āptopadeśhavakyam śabdah*: which means that the teachings of Siddha Purushas (perfected souls) have a probative force and this is technically known as Shabda Pramana (verbal evidence). Rishi Jaimini, the commentator, says that such Apta Purushas (authorities) may be born among the Aryans and the Mlechchhas.[4]

The preface that Vivekananda wrote to his translation of *The Imitation of Christ* is important because, besides being his earliest written work (1889), four years before he spoke at the Parliament, it reflects faithfully the features of Christianity that he found attractive. He could understand and identify with the author of this work, whose ideals and way of life closely resembled the aspirations and values of a traditional Hindu renunciant (*samnyāsin*). Vivekananda admired the author's radical renunciation, his thirst for purity, and his unceasing spiritual effort (*sādhana*).

Vivekananda likened *The Imitation of Christ* to the *Bhagavadgītā* in its spirit of complete self-surrender and saw the author as embodying the Hindu ideal of devotion to God as a servant to a master (*dāsya bhakti*). We see in this preface what would be a central theme of Vivekananda's Christology—Jesus as the model embodiment of renunciation.

Vivekananda presented his most detailed understanding of Jesus in a lecture entitled, "Christ, The Messenger," delivered in Los Angeles in 1900. In this lecture the core components of his Christology are identified and we will now consider the salient aspects.

Jesus: The Otherworldly Renunciant

Vivekananda represents Jesus as entirely otherworldly, with no interest in this "evanescent world and its belongings."[5] He is critical of interpreters who have spoken of Jesus as a politician, a patriotic Jew, or even a military leader. The Gospels, according to Vivekananda, offer no justification for such readings. He cites Matthew 8:20, "The foxes have holes, the birds of the air have nests, but the Son of man hath not where to lay his head," as the best commentary on the life of Jesus. He speaks of Jesus as a "disembodied, unfettered, unbound spirit," with no consciousness of the physical body.

> He had no sex ideas! He was a soul! Nothing but a soul–just working a body for the good of humanity; and that was all his relation to the body. In the soul there is no sex. The disembodied soul has no relationship to the animal, no relationship to the body. The ideal may be far away beyond us. But never mind, keep to the ideal. Let us confess that it is our ideal, but we cannot approach it yet.[6]

Christ, according to Vivekananda, was a *samnyāsin* (renunciant) and his teachings were meant to be followed only by *samnyāsins*. The world and life in the world, says Vivekananda, had no interest for Jesus. His only concern was to push it forward towards God and to enable everyone to realize their spiritual nature.[7]

It was on the subject of renunciation that Vivekananda's disappointment with the dichotomy between ideal and practice in Christianity became most evident. He felt strongly that Christians had strayed far from the ideals of Jesus. In the city of Detroit on February 21, 1894, Vivekananda was fiery and eloquent, and held before his audience the model of Jesus as renunciant (*samnyāsin*).

> You are not Christians. No, as a nation you are not. Go back to Christ. Go back to him who had nowhere to lay his head. "The birds have their nests and the beasts their lairs, but the Son of Man has nowhere to lay his

> head." Yours is religion preached in the name of luxury. What an irony of fate! Reverse this if you want to live, reverse this. It is all hypocrisy that I have heard in this country. All this prosperity, all this from Christ! Christ would have denied all such heresies. If you can join these two, this wonderful prosperity with the ideal of Christ, it is well. But if you cannot, better go back to him and give this up. Better be ready to live in rags with Christ than to live in palaces without him.[8]

Jesus: The Ahistorical Teacher

Swami Vivekananda's characterization of Jesus as the teacher of a doctrine of otherworldliness is connected closely with another significant dimension of his Christology. This is his almost complete disinterest in the historical Jesus, a subject of central concern for the Christian tradition. In response to a question about the crucifixion of Jesus, his answer was direct and terse: "Christ was God incarnate; they could not crucify him. That which was crucified was only a semblance, a mirage."[9] Vivekananda seemed well aware of some of the scholarly disputes about the historical Jesus, but attributes no significance to these. He spends little time wondering why this may be important to the Christian tradition. Historical truths appear to him to be nonessential. Vivekananda does not question Jesus's historicity, but attributes no special significance to the connection between history and his religious significance.

> We are not here to discuss how much of the New Testament is true, we are not here to discuss how much of that life is historical. It does not matter at all whether the New Testament was written within five hundred years of his birth, nor does it matter even, *how much of that life is true.* But there is something behind it, something we want to imitate.[10]

Although Vivekananda is not interested in Christian claims for the historical Jesus, he is concerned to argue for the Asiatic nature of Christ. This is an idea that Vivekananda inherited from the Brahmo Samaj leaders, Ram Mohan Roy and Keshub Chandra Sen. Although the historical origin of the idea of the Asiatic Christ is difficult to trace, Keshub Chandra Sen articulated it most forcefully. Sen obviously included the Middle East in his geographical definition of "Asia"; his point is to claim Jesus for Asia and to employ this as an argument to contest western claims of superiority in relation to people from Asia. While denigrating people of Asian origin, westerners are, in fact, following an Asian teacher. In a famous lecture, "Jesus Christ: Europe and Asia," delivered in 1866, Sen spoke of the Asiatic Christ.

> I rejoice, yea, I am proud, that I am an Asiatic. And was not Jesus Christ an Asiatic? Yes and his disciples were Asiatics, and in Asia. When I

> reflect on this, my love for Jesus becomes a hundredfold intensified; I feel him nearer to my heart, and deeper in my national sympathies. Why should I then feel ashamed to acknowledge that nationality which he acknowledged? Shall I not rather say, he is more congenial and akin to my oriental nature, more agreeable to my oriental habits of thought and feeling? And is it not true that an Asiatic can read the imageries and allegories of the Gospel, and its descriptions of natural sceneries, of customs and manners, with greater interest, and a fuller perception of their force and beauty, than Europeans?[11]

Vivekananda speaks of Jesus as a "true son of the Orient," possessing what he describes as a preference for the practical in matters of religion. Echoing the words of Keshub Chandra Sen, Vivekananda speaks in almost identical terms about Jesus's identity.

> Many times you forget, also, that the Nazarene himself was still an Oriental. With all your attempts to paint him with blue eyes and yellow hair, the Nazarene was still an Oriental. All the similes, the imageries, in which the Bible is written –— the scenes, the locations, the attitudes, the groups, the poetry and symbol — speak to you of the Orient: of the bright sky, of the heat, of the sun, of the desert, of the thirsty men and animals; of men and women coming with pitchers on their heads to fill them at the wells; of the flocks, of the ploughmen, of the cultivation that is going on around; of the water-mill and wheel, of the mill-pond, of the mill-stones. All these are to be seen today in Asia.[12]

The affirmation of Jesus's Asiatic identity was important to Swami Vivekananda because it enabled him to claim that Jesus is better understood in India than in the western world. It was the ground also for challenging the Eurocentric focus of Christianity and arguing for the superiority of Asia in religious matters, in spite of western political and military might.

> Who are following the teachings of the Gita? — the Europeans. And who are acting according to the will of Jesus Christ? — the descendants of Shri Krishna.[13]

In speaking of Europeans as followers of the *Bhagavadgītā*, Vivekananda had in mind the teaching of the text on the necessity for action in the world. Krishna called on Arjuna to overcome cowardice and to be strong and brave on the field of battle. Vivekananda felt that such qualities were seen more in the lives of Europeans. Jesus, on the other hand, taught a doctrine of world renunciation, more faithfully followed by Hindus.

Jesus: The *Advaitin*

Swami Vivekananda's otherworldly Jesus, whose significance will not be found in the facts of history, was preeminently a teacher of Advaita. Vivekananda's Christology was informed decisively by his theory of human religious evolution. The world of religions is, as he puts it, "only a travelling, a coming up of different men and women, through various conditions and circumstances to the same goal."[14] For Vivekananda, the goal of this journey is the awakening to the nondual reality underlying the universe and constituting the self (*ātmā*) of all. This awakening is available in all the religions of the world. Paths may be different, but the goal of nonduality is one and the same.

Vivekananda traces three stages in the development of all religions. In the first stage, God is understood as an extra-cosmic being, both omnipotent and omniscient. There is little human intimacy with God at this stage, and the emphasis is on divine transcendence. The second stage emphasizes panentheism. God is understood to be present not only in the heavens, but also in our world and, most importantly, in the human being. In the final stage of religious evolution, the human being discovers unity and identity with the all-pervasive, nondual truth of the universe. All religions, according to Vivekananda, reflect these three phases, since the evolution to a higher stage does not imply the discarding of any earlier phase.

Employing the Hindu teaching about *adhikāribheda* or the necessity of a teacher to relate his teaching to a student's religious aptitude, Vivekananda reads Jesus as teaching to three distinct types of disciples.

> To the masses who could not conceive anything higher than a Personal God, he said, "Pray to your Father in Heaven." To others who could grasp a higher idea, he said, "I am the vine you are the branches," but to his disciples to whom he revealed himself more fully, he proclaimed the highest truth, "I and my Father are One."[15]

The dualistic teachings of Jesus, according to Vivekananda, were meant for the uneducated masses, who could not understand a higher teaching. He felt that his theory of religious evolution from dualism to nondualism was alone capable of explaining apparent contradictions in Christian teachings. It helps us to reconcile the teaching of Jesus that the kingdom of heaven is within us and his instruction to pray to the Father in heaven. These are not meant, according to Vivekananda, for the same person.

Given Swami Vivekananda's overall view of human religiosity as culminating in nonduality and his understanding of Jesus as a teacher of this truth, it does not surprise that he gives particular importance to the Gospel of John, and especially to those statements of Jesus that affirm unity with God and the realization of God within. The two most often cited by him are the John 10:30 text, "The Father and I are one," and the Luke 17:21 text, "The Kingdom of Heaven is among you." He interprets "I and My Father are one, "to have the same meaning as the Advaita great sentences (*mahāvākyas*) such as "I am *brahman* (*aham brahmāsmi*)."[16] His Christology is decisively shaped by the significance that he gives especially to the texts from John. He spoke of the essence of Christianity as contained in the first five verses of John.[17]

JESUS: THE *AVATĀRA* OR *JĪVANMUKTA*?

Swami Vivekananda turns to the *Bhagavadgītā* teaching about the incarnation of God (*avatāra*) to explain the nature of Jesus. He cites well-known verses from the fourth chapter (6-8):

> Though I am unborn, of changeless nature, and Lord of beings, yet subjugating My Prakriti, I come into being by my own Maya.
>
> Whenever virtue subsides and immortality prevails, then I body Myself forth. For the protection of the good, for the destruction of the wicked, and for the establishment of Dharma, I come into being in every age.[18]

We must, however, qualify Jesus's nature as divine incarnation in several important respects.

First, Vivekananda argues strongly for the multiplicity of divine incarnations and against the Christian claim for the singleness and uniqueness of Jesus. He saw the belief in a single incarnation as a limit imposed on God. This is repeated often in his discussion of Jesus.

> The great limitation Christians have is that they do not heed other manifestations of God besides Christ. He was a manifestation of God; so was Buddha; so were some others, and there will be hundreds of others. Do not limit God anywhere.[19]

He exhorted his Los Angeles audience in 1900 to find God "not only in Jesus of Nazareth, but in all the great Ones that have preceded him, in all that came after him, and all that are yet to come."[20] In articulating this argument for multiple divine incarnations, Vivekananda enunciates an important general principle. This is the idea that whatever happens once in nature, must have happened before and will repeat again in the future (CW 4: 151). Singularity, in other words, is not the mark of truth. Diana Eck speaks of the valuing of singularity in religion as the "myth of monotheism," and sees this as pervasive in the monotheistic traditions of Judaism, Christianity and Islam.[21]

Second, although employing the traditional terminology of the *avatāra*, Vivekananda's understanding of the doctrine may not be the traditional one as expounded, for example, by a classical Vaiṣṇava theologian like Rāmānuja. He speaks often of the worship of God as a human being in language that suggests this to be a concession to human need. There are, according to Vivekananda, only two types of human beings who do not worship God as human: the human brute and the *yogī* of the highest kind. The brute has no religion and the *yogī* has gone beyond the limits of human nature. Everyone else is constrained to worship God as human.

> However much you may try by struggle, by abstraction, by whatsoever method you like, still so long as you are man in the world of men, your world is human, your religion is human, and your God is human.[22]

And further,

> If I, as an Oriental, have to worship Jesus of Nazareth, there is only one way left to me, that is, to worship him as God and nothing else.[23]

Descriptions like these suggest clearly that the perception and worship of the human as God is a reflection of the limits and necessity of human nature. Even as a buffalo will imagine and see God only as a huge buffalo, or a fish only as a huge fish, we must see God as human. Although not necessarily ruling out the more traditional doctrine of God becoming a special human being, Vivekananda's epistemological argument places the initiative on the human side of the equation.

Third, and perhaps most important of all for his Advaita Christology, Jesus, like the Buddha, represents a state to be attained. In 1895, during an address at the Thousand Island Park in New York, Vivekananda spoke clearly on this:

> The Absolute cannot be worshipped, so we must worship a manifestation, such a one as has our nature. Jesus had our nature; he became the Christ; so can we, and so *must* we. Christ and Buddha were the names of a state to be attained; Jesus and Gautama were the persons to manifest it.[24]

Jesus became the Christ and Gautama the Buddha. It is the state that is important and not the historical person. The state is universal and eternal and not so the historical particularities of the person who attains it.

One of the paramount errors of the Christian tradition in history, according to Swami Vivekananda, is that the messenger became the message. Christians lacked the insight to separate these two and the messenger, who cared not to be remembered or known, took center stage. The aim of Christian life should not be to imitate Jesus, but to be Jesus. The potential to be as great as Jesus or Buddha is inherent in every human being. In Advaita terms, Jesus is more appropriately described as *jīvanmukta,* and not *avatāra.* The *jīvanmukta* (living free) is a human being who has attained liberation (*mokṣa*). In the Advaita (nondual) tradition, liberation is the consequence of understanding the identity of the self (*ātmā*) with the Infinite (*brahman*). Such living liberation is a possibility for all human beings. The *avatāra*, on the other hand, is understood traditionally to be a descent of the divine into the world.

Speaking of Christ as a universal state of being and of Jesus as someone who had perfectly realized this state and whose role in life was to help others attain this state, enabled Swami Vivekananda to challenge and to recast the traditional Christian understanding of the human problem as one of sin. He reads John 29: "Behold the Lamb of God, which taketh away the sin of the world," to mean that Christ shows us the way to become perfect. "God," says Vivekananda, "became Christ to show man his true nature, that we too are God. We are human coverings over the Divine; but as the divine Man, Christ and we are one."[25] The problem is not sin but, in Advaita terminology, *avidyā* (ignorance) of our true nature.

> The Vedānta recognizes no sin, it only recognizes error. And the greatest error, says the Vedānta, is to say that you are weak, that you are a sinner, a miserable creature, and that you have no power and you cannot do this and that.[26]

Vivekananda never missed an opportunity to question the Christian doctrine of original sin and to compare it with the Advaita understanding of the inherent purity of the *ātmā.* He felt that the Christian tradition emphasized, too much, human depravity and sinfulness.

> Be not deluded by your religion teaching original sin, for the same religion teaches original purity. When Adam fell, he fell from purity. Purity is our real nature and to regain that is the object of all religion.[27]

It does not surprise us that Swami Vivekananda exemplified minimal interest in the crucifixion and resurrection of Jesus or in Christian teaching about atonement. Atonement, or the claim that the death of Jesus opened the doorway to salvation, made no sense in the worldview of Vivekananda. Liberation (*moḳsa*), in Advaita teaching, is the result of self-knowledge and cannot be attained by an action done by someone else. He expressed abhorrence at the idea of salvation gained through the shedding of blood and left no doubt about his strong feelings on such a teaching.

> If anyone would come to me and say, "Be saved by my blood," I would say to him, "My brother, go away; I will go to hell; I am not a coward to take innocent blood to go to heaven; I am ready for hell."[28]

Vivekananda's Advaita Christology: Limits and Insights

- **Vivekananda's Hierarchy of Religions**

 In offering an assessment of the Advaita Christology of Swami Vivekananda, we must clarify the nature of his reading of the Christian tradition. Vivekananda does not set out to interpret the meaning of the Christian tradition in the manner of a systematic Christian theologian or a biblical scholar. He has a clearly developed theoretical framework through which he reads the history of human religiosity and applies this to his understanding of Hindu and non-Hindu traditions. At the core of his approach is his view that religions reflect an evolutionary progression from dualism to panentheism that culminates in nondualism. Nondualism (Advaita) is the fulfillment and culmination of the human religious quest. From the panoramic vantage point of this Advaita theology of religions, Swami Vivekananda surveys the Christian tradition and interprets it in the light of his evolutionary theology. What Swami Vivekananda offers us is an Advaita view of Christianity that conforms to his understanding of religious evolution. As one commentator observed, "If Christians can speak of an unknown Christ of Hinduism, Hindus can speak of an unknown Vedānta of Christianity."[29]

- **Vivekananda's Inclusive Theology of Religions**

 Inclusive theologies of religion, whether of the Advaita or other varieties, have much that we can commend, but are not exempt from significant problems. On the positive side, the inclusivist avoids the condemnation of religions in their entirety. Religions, Vivekananda teaches, are not moving from error to truth but from lower truth to higher truth, and these truths serve the needs of persons at different levels of growth. These teachings should be accepted and not condemned.[30]

 > To the Hindu, man is not traveling from error to truth, but from truth to truth, from lower to higher truth. To him all the religions, from the lowest fetishism to the highest absolutism, mean so many attempts of the human soul to grasp and realize the Infinite, each

> determined by the conditions of its birth and association, and each of these marks a stage of progress.[31]

> All religions are so many stages. Each of them represents the stage through which the human soul passes to realize God. Therefore, not one of them should be neglected. None of these stages are dangerous or bad. They are good. Just as a child becomes a young man, and a young man becomes an old man, so these are travelling from truth to truth; they become dangerous only when they become rigid, and will not move further—when he ceases to grow.[32]

On the problematic side, however, inclusivism often speaks of the meaning of another tradition in a language not recognized in the self-understanding of its practitioners. Even as the Hindu will find it difficult to understand the claim of some Christians that Jesus Christ is the goal and fulfillment of the Hindu religious quest, some Christians find it difficult to see the fulfillment of their religious quest in Advaita. Hindu dualists (*Dvaitins*) and qualified nondualists (*Viśiṣṭādvaitins*) will also question the assumption that their traditions culminate in nonduality and that "dualism naturally appeals to less educated minds."[33] It is important to add, however, that Swami Vivekananda's proposition that all religions culminate in Advaita does not imply any program of proselytization to bring this about. For him, it is a natural theological evolution ongoing within each tradition in its own distinctive manner. For Vivekananda, Advaita is not an exclusive Hindu teaching, but one that is available in all traditions. As he put it,

> The Christian is not become a Hindu or a Buddhist; nor the Hindu nor the Buddhist to become a Christian. But each religion must assimilate the others and yet preserve its own individuality and grow according to its own law of growth.[34]

Inclusivism sustains itself through a selective reading of the texts of a tradition. Swami Vivekananda, as we noted earlier, gives extraordinary importance to two texts: "The John 10:30 text, 'The Father and I are one,' and the Luke 17:21 text, 'The Kingdom of Heaven is among you.'" On the basis of these two texts, he speaks of Jesus as a teacher of Advaita. It is indeed possible to read these texts as conveying the deepest insights of the Advaita tradition, but this is not how the Christian tradition has interpreted their meaning. The often quoted "The Father and I are one," is read within the tradition as speaking to the nature of Jesus as incarnation and not as affirming a truth valid for all human beings. It is not clear also how the disciples of Jesus, hearing these statements, would grasp the meaning of the identity of *ātmā* and *brahman* as taught in the *Upaniṣads*. If Advaita is the highest teaching of Jesus, it is not unreasonable to expect that the Christian textual evidence should be more substantial.

- **Advaita: Ontology and Methodology**

From the Advaita side of the equation, Advaita is both an understanding of the nature of reality as well as a distinctive methodology of instruction about this. There are two truth claims that are fundamental to Advaita. First, is the identity of the individual self (*ātmā*) with the limitless *brahman*. This is the teaching enunciated in the great sentences (*mahāvākyas*) of the *Upaniṣads*: "That Thou Art (*tat tvam asi*)" is taken from *Chāndogya Upaniṣad* 6.8.7 of the *Sāma Veda*; "This *ātmā* is *brahma* (*ayam ātmā brahma*)" is taken from the *Māṇḍukya Upanisad* 2 of the *Atharva Veda*; "Awareness is *brahma* (*prajñānaṁ brahma*)" is taken from the *Aitareya Upaniṣad* 5.3 of the *Ṛg Veda*; and "I am *brahma* (*ahaṁ brahmāsmi*)" is taken from *Bṛhadāraṇyaka Upaniṣad* 1.4.10 of the *Yajur Veda*. Each of these sentences is interpreted by Advaita commentators as teaching the unity of the self (*ātmā*) and the Infinite (*brahman*). This is the core of Advaita instruction and the sine qua non for liberation in the Vedantic tradition.

The second claim, just as important and fundamental to Advaita, is that *brahman* constitutes the truth (*satya*) of the universe, even as clay is the truth of all objects made of clay. This is articulated in the famous text from *Chāndogya Upaniṣad* (3.14.1), "*sarvam khalvidam brahma* (All this indeed is the infinite)." This second truth is necessary for ensuring that Advaita does not culminate in the affirmation of a *brahman* world dualism and for ensuring that the limitless nature of *brahman* is not compromised. We do not see any evidence of this in the teachings of Jesus, and Swami Vivekananda does not cite any Christian texts to validate this Advaita teaching in Christianity. In addition, we do not see any evidence of Advaita methods of teaching in Christianity as we see in the *Upaniṣads*. Such methods include the knower-known distinction, the analysis of the three states of experiences, and the cause-effect relationship. The knower-known distinction points to the self as the subject consciousness. It is the awareness because of which the body, senses and mind are objectified and known. The analysis of the three states of experience (waking, dream, sleep) is intended to establish that the self as consciousness is present in all states. There is no time when the self is not. The cause-effect analysis explains that the effect (world) is a name and form manifestation of the cause (*brahman*). The cause does not exist separately or independently from the effect.[35]

- **The Significance of Tradition and Interpretation**

  Swami Vivekananda, like Hindu interpreters before and after him, including Ram Mohan Roy, Keshub Chandra Sen, Gandhi and Radhakrishnan, did not depend on Christian theological interpretations for their understanding of Jesus. Instead, a deliberate effort is made to distinguish and to separate Jesus from Christianity and to offer an interpretation of his significance in the categories of the Hindu tradition. This separation of Jesus from Christianity allows Swami Vivekananda to interpret Jesus's teachings in the light of Advaita. Such interpretations can be insightful and enriching, as well as risky. Readings of a tradition by an outsider, bypassing all the layers of tradition, may bring fresh and novel perspectives enabling insiders to see new and overlooked dimensions. Swami Vivekananda's reading of the John 10:30 text in Advaita terms may be one such example. At the same time, ignoring or treating a tradition as unnecessary for understanding the meaning of its most important teacher risks the offering of interpretations that are never recognized as credible within the tradition and have no impact on that tradition's self-understanding. Matters that are important and critical to Christian understanding of Jesus such as his historicity, death, and resurrection, are not given significance. A parallel situation may be a Christian reading of the *Upaniṣads* minus engagement with the traditional Advaita teachers (*ācāryas*) and the historical community (*sampradāya*) that have preserved, transmitted, and enriched this teaching.

- **The Centrality of *Anubhava***

  Swami Vivekananda's Advaita Christology rests also on a fundamental pillar of his understanding of religion. At the heart of what is important in religion are not doctrines, dogmas or theological traditions, but direct, self-certifying religious experience that he refers to as *anubhava*. Religious certitude will not be found in scriptures or institutions but in religious experience. Vivekananda speaks of this religious experience as the Christ state. It is universally accessible and not identical with the historical Jesus. Jesus attained this state, but so can all human beings:

  > But if you go to the fountain-head of Christianity, you will find that it is based upon experience. Christ said that he saw God; the disciples said they felt God; and so forth. Similarly, in Buddhism, it is

> Buddha's experience. He experienced certain truths, saw them, came in contact with them, and preached them to the world. Thus, it is clear that all the religions of the world have been built upon that one universal and adamantine foundation of all our knowledge-direct experience.[36]

Vivekananda understood religion as mystical experience and this explains why he was uninterested in the historical Jesus, his birth, death, and resurrection. He was also indifferent to institutional Christianity and its traditions. For Vivekananda, none of these are essential for getting to the true meaning of Jesus. In contrast to Mahatma Gandhi's understanding of Jesus, the social dimension of the teachings of Jesus also failed to engage him. The one teaching of Jesus that Vivekananda elevated to a great height above all other things, was the one Vivekananda believed to be an expression of Advaita.

Conclusion

I have identified many critical questions prompted by Swami Vivekananda's Advaita Christology from both the Advaita and Christian traditions. At the same time, we must take note of the distinctive insights and challenges offered by his Christology. On the Advaita side, it presents the claim that the fundamental insight of the tradition about the *ātmā-brahman* identity is available in other traditions. He universalizes Advaita in a way not done before. On the Christian side, Vivekananda suggests that there may be a distinctive Advaita way of understanding the nature of Jesus's unity with God, that could enrich Christian theological understanding. His effort was also directed to universalizing the meaning of Jesus beyond the boundaries of Christianity. Although Vivekananda may have exaggerated Jesus's otherworldliness and his disinterest in this world, Vivekananda's reminder to Christians that Jesus gave a message of renunciation, critical to all authentic religion, is one that cannot be ignored. Vivekananda also problematized and contested Christian understandings of Jesus as the exclusive revelation of God and savior of humanity. Many contemporary Christian theologians have recognized the problems of such claims for Jesus and have responded with new theologies of religion.[37] The role of Jesus as teacher or *guru* was primary for Swami Vivekananda. In the Christian tradition, broadly speaking, the emphasis is more upon the nature of Jesus and less on his role as teacher. Swami Vivekananda's observation that the messenger became the message is a valuable insight that may lead to the recovery of the significance of Jesus the teacher and his teachings.

References

1. The text is from Luke 9:18. It is question addressed by Jesus to his disciples.
2. David Kopf, *The Brahmo Samaj and the Shaping of the Modern Indian Mind* (New Jersey: Princeton University Press, 1979), 205. Sen broke from the Brahmo Samaj and launched The New Dispensation (Nava Vidhan) in 1878, believing that he had a new revelation to harmonize all conflicting creeds.
3. All references are taken from *The Complete Works of Swami Vivekananda.*
4. CW 8: 160-161.
5. CW 4: 144
6. CW 4: 145
7. CW 4: 146
8. CW 8: 213
9. CW 1: 328
10. CW 4: 146. Emphasis added. It is of interest to note that Swami Vivekananda dismissed Nicholas Notovich's view that Jesus traveled to Tibet and was buried there after his death. See CW 6: 359; CW 3: 264.
11. S. D. Collett, ed., *Lectures and Tracts by Keshub Chunder Sen* (London: Strahan, 1870), 33-34.
12. CW 4: 142
13. CW 5: 454
14. CW 1: 18.
15. CW 2: 143
16. Texts taken from *The New Oxford Annotated Bible* (New York, Oxford University Press, 1991).
17. CW 7:3
18. CW 4: 151-152
19. CW 4: 31
20. CW 4: 152
21. Eck, *Encountering God* (Boston: Beacon Press, 1993), 59.
22. CW 4: 140
23. CW 4: 147
24. CW 7: 29
25. CW 7: 4
26. CW 2: 295
27. CW 7: 418
28. CW 8: 209
29. M. M. Thomas, *The Acknowledged Christ of the Indian Renaissance*, 150.
30. CW 4: 147

31 CW 1: 17

32 CW 2: 500

33 CW 2: 141

34 CW 1: 24

35 I have discussed these methods in detail elsewhere. See Anantanand Rambachan, *The Advaita Worldview: God, World and Humanity* (Albany: State University of New York Press, 2015).

36 CW 1:126

37 See, for example, the excellent survey by Paul F. Knitter, *Introducing Theologies of Religions* (Maryknoll: Orbis Books, 2002).

CHAPTER SEVEN

INTERRELIGIOUS RELATIONS AS FRIENDSHIP: MAHATMA GANDHI AND CHARLES FREER ANDREWS

The Ideal of Friendship

Friendship (*maitrī*) is a relationship that is highly valued and commended in the traditions of Hinduism. In fact, friendship is an ideal towards which we ought to aspire in all our relationships. In the *Bhagavadgītā* (12:13-20), Krishna offers a detailed description of the human being who is dear to him. He describes this person as one who is free from hatred, who is a friend to all beings, compassionate, nonpossessive, free from self-centeredness, and forgiving. As is clear in this description from the *Bhagavadgītā*, friendship has both a negative and positive character. Negatively, it signifies freedom from hate. Positively, friendship implies a value for the other, along with compassion and a forgiving disposition. In the vision of the *Bhagavadgītā*, one who has attained the ideal of friendship transcends the dualism of friend and enemy, and sees all beings with the vision of friendship. Such a person is free from hostile attitudes towards others and is described as "the same with reference to an enemy and friend, and in honor and disgrace" (*Bhagavadgītā* 12:18). The fulfillment of friendship in the Hindu tradition is the overcoming of the division of the world into friends and enemies, those who are loved and those who are hated and despised. The terminology of "friend" and "friendship" is retained, but is given new meaning by including all beings (*sarvabhūtānāṁ*).

Friendship and the Unity of Existence

At the heart of the ideal of an all-inclusive friendship is the teaching that the infinite *brahman* exists identically in all beings. Since the infinite is present in each being as the warp and woof of selfhood, to see the infinite in another is to see oneself in another. To be hostile to and alienated from another, is to deny and reject oneself. As the *Īśa Upaniṣad* (6) puts it, "One who sees all beings in the Self and the Self in all beings does not hate." Hate arises from the condition of ignorance (*avidyā*), which is a blindness to the unity and identity of the infinite in all beings. The unliberated divides the world into friends and enemies, but the liberated sees only with the eyes of friendship. Appreciating the nature of ignorance, and its potency to distort our view of reality, the liberated sees only with compassion (*karuṇa*). This does not unrealistically deny the possibility of differing viewpoints or even the necessity to oppose and struggle against another. Wisdom, however, enables us to see ourselves in the other, the one with whom we disagree and with whom we may be locked in struggle. We cannot dehumanize the one in whom we see ourselves or rejoice in his humiliation. We see this method in action in the case of Gandhi. Even in the midst of the strongest disagreements, Gandhi never sought to win support for his case by demonizing his opponent. He understood clearly that when a conflict is constructed sharply in terms of "we" and "they," "friend" and "enemy," "victory" and "defeat," the doors to reconciliation and a transformed community are shut. One is left with an enemy, a defeated enemy perhaps, and the next round of the conflict is only postponed. Gandhi included the opponent in the circle of his friendship and identity, his "we." Friendship, in the highest sense, is the overcoming of alienation and estrangement from others through the recognition of one's own self, the infinite *brahman*, in the other.

Attaining this ideal of friendship is undoubtedly challenging. The principal obstacle, from the perspective of the Hindu tradition, is our non-recognition of the culturally and socially constructed nature of the many identities that we profess and our tendency to regard these as absolute and unchanging. Such identities may be constructed on the basis of race, ethnicity, culture and, in the case of many Hindus, caste. Such identities are then opposed to other similarly constructed but different identities that are regarded as inferior. Having a distinctive cultural identity is not problematic, but the devaluation of others certainly is. Such ways of seeing obscure the fundamental and unconstructed identity that all human beings share— the unity of self in the infinite. In the case of caste identity, for example, one professes an identity that is hierarchically related to other identities and that limited one's ability to form friendships with others who are regarded as impure. The liberated vision in the Hindu tradition is incompatible with such caste-based identities and requires their overcoming through self-understanding.

It must be emphasized, however, that this understanding of the unity of self is not opposed to the multiplicity of particular identities, provided these do not dehumanize and demean those who do not share these and do not limit our ability to enter into relationships of friendship. The problem is non-recognition of the more fundamental identity that is shared and that is the ground and possibility of all particular identities. Particular constructed identities must not obscure the universal identity that the Hindu tradition sees at the heart of the universe. I am reminded here of the words in Galatians 3:28, "There is no longer Jew or Greek, there is no longer slave or free, there is no longer male and female; for all of you are one in Christ Jesus." Without ignoring the specific context of these words, they speak powerfully also to the Hindu if the word *brahman* is substituted for "Christ Jesus." There is and is not a Jew, Greek, male and female.

Tulasidasa on Friendship: Shared Identity, Virtue, Trust, and Generosity

Friendship describes the character of the relationship that we establish with others when our understanding is centered on life's unity and the indivisibility of the infinite. What are the features of such a relationship? What are its defining characteristics? To answer this question, I turn to the sixteenth century poet-saint Tulasidasa and his version of the Rāmāyaṇa (Rāmacaritamānas). In the Kiṣkindhākaṇḍa (Book 4) of his text, Tulasidasa characterizes friendship as having a fourfold character and I will note each one in turn.

The first is a shared identity expressing in compassion or concern for the other. Tulasidasa describes a friend as experiencing sorrow when his friend is in sorrow. In fact, he goes on to add that, in the eyes of a friend, the other's sorrow, even though like a grain of sand, is always mountain-like in dimensions. Tulasidasa seems to be suggesting here that the ground of friendship is identification with another. One includes the other in one's understanding of oneself in a manner that makes the suffering of the other a matter of concern and urgency. One cannot be a friend and be indifferent to the well-being of the other.

Second, according to Tulasidasa, friendship implies mutual ethical responsibilities. Friends feel morally responsible for each other and are committed to each other's moral well-being. Friends care about each other's ethical health.

Third, friendship is a relationship of mutual trust; it excludes suspicion about the other's motivation. He illustrates his understanding of the meaning of trust in friendship by explaining that a friend speaks publicly only about the virtues of the other. Trust means freedom from the desire to humiliate or demean.

Fourth, friendship is generosity. Friends give and receive without anxiety. The anxiety mentioned here is the fear that one will not receive equal value for what is given. In friendship, there are times when one may give more and receive less, or when one may receive more and give less, but friends do not keep records of what is given and received. Record-keeping signifies a different kind of relationship. For Tulasidasa, therefore, friendship signifies a relationship infused with compassion, ethical obligations, trust and generosity.

Gandhi and C.F. Andrews: Interreligious Friendship

If we employ this fourfold characterization of friendship by Tulasidasa, how does it illumine our understanding of the promises and challenges of friendship across religious traditions? We will examine Tulasidasa's four characteristics in the light of the friendship between Mahatma Gandhi (1869-1948) and his closest Christian friend, Charles Freer Andrews (1871-1940).

Andrews was the son of a Christian minister belonging to the Catholic Apostolic Church, but later joined the Church of England. He was ordained as a priest in 1897 and moved to Delhi, India, in 1904, to teach at St. Stephen's College. In 1914, Andrews responded to a call from the Indian nationalist leader, Gopal Krishna Gokhale, for volunteers to help Gandhi in his struggle on behalf of indentured Indian laborers in South Africa. From 1914, until his death in 1940, Andrews worked closely with Gandhi in the Indian independence movement and in the service of India. He was perhaps Gandhi's closest friend and certainly the only person to call the Mahatma by his first name "Mohan." Gandhi, in turn, addressed him as "Charlie." Their friendship blossomed quickly and remains an illuminating example of a relationship across religious traditions. Andrews spent one month with Gandhi in South Africa. His note to Gandhi after his departure speaks for itself about the depth of their relationship.

> It was so like you to be occupied in dear acts of service for my voyage. I didn't quite know how much you had learnt to love me till that morning when you put your hand on my shoulder and spoke of the loneliness that there would be to you when I was gone. When I saw you on the wharf, standing with hands raised in benediction, I knew, as I had not known, even in Pretoria, how very, very dear you have become to me.[1]

Shared Identity

Compassion as a quality of a human relationship is grounded in a discernment of some shared identity. This opens up the possibility of sharing the suffering and joy of another. In the case of religious traditions, this shared identity consists often in the sense of belonging to a community that is defined by allegiance to a person, specific doctrines or rituals. Boundaries are forged from shared doctrines or loyalty to a founder/teacher. We identify strongly with those sharing this identity, speak out when we feel that their rights are infringed, and empathize with their suffering and joy. We are not always as attentive and responsive to the condition of those who we define, theologically or otherwise, as being outside the boundaries of our community of identity.

In the case of friendship across religious traditions, common doctrine and ritual may not be sources for a shared identity that enable the flourishing of empathy. If caring about another is a vital feature of interreligious friendships, the elements of our shared identity that enable these to flourish will have to be identified and affirmed. In interreligious relationships, identity with others cannot be contingent on a change in the other's identity or self-understanding. The shared identity that we affirm must allow the other the freedom to be different.

In the case of the Hindu tradition, the ground of identity with a person of another religious tradition is the equal and identical existence of the infinite one in all. One recognizes oneself in the other. Shared doctrines and rituals foster community and friendship, but there is an inclusive identity that disposes us positively to the other, overcomes the idea of the other as a stranger, and inspires us to form relationships of friendship. The important question that must engage us all is the following. Why is the person of another religious tradition important and valuable to me? Why should I extend to one the embrace of friendship? What is the shared identity that includes one?

Gandhi and Andrews differed considerably in background and training. Andrews was British and belonged to the nation that exercised imperial rule over India. Gandhi was Indian and led a struggle against British rule in India. Andrews was Christian; Gandhi was Hindu. Andrews was trained for the Christian ministry; Gandhi was educated as a lawyer. Gandhi's opening words in an article that he wrote after Andrew's death provide insight about their attraction to each other.

> Nobody, probably, knew Charlie Andrews as well as I did. When we met in South Africa we simply met as brothers and remained as such to the

> end. It was not a friendship between an Englishman and an Indian. It was an unbreakable bond between two seekers and servants.[2]

Gandhi and Andrews were both deeply committed to their respective religious traditions and their primary motivation in life was religious. They saw in each other, however, an earnest fellow seeker after God. For Gandhi, God or Truth was always beyond full human comprehension and our understanding was ever evolving.

> If we had attained the full vision of Truth, we would no longer be mere seekers, but have become one with God, for Truth is God. But being only seekers, we prosecute our quest, and are conscious of our imperfection. And if we are imperfect ourselves, religion as conceived by us must also be imperfect. We have not realized religion in its perfection, even as we have not realized God. Religion of our conception, being thus imperfect, is always subject to a process of evolution.[3]

Gandhi thought of himself as an earnest seeker, searching out fellow seekers in all traditions, learning from them and seeing with greater clarity his own errors. This is what drove him to seek friends across religious boundaries.

Andrews's journey to India helped him to see the limits of his theology, to discern God in the teachings and practices of Hindus, and to be open to the wisdom of the Hinduism.

> The world's great religious literature has now been opened to our gaze, and we find that this inner vision and these supreme moments of exaltation are not confined within the boundaries of Christendom. It is impossible, for instance, to read the vital spiritual experiences told by men and women in India, especially the religious folk-songs of the peasant mystics, without coming to that conclusion.[4]

The shared quality of openness to deeper understandings of religious truth was complemented by a concern on the part of both men to live their lives as servants of the poor and the oppressed. This is what first attracted Andrews to Gandhi when he learned of Gandhi's work in South Africa. Andrews had the experience of serving industrial workers in the slums of London. He saw Christ in the suffering Indians in South Africa and in the untouchables of India. For Gandhi, whose ultimate aim in life was to know God, a life of service was indispensable. One finds God by seeing God in creation and becoming one with it. This is possible only through service. "I am endeavoring to see God through service of humanity," wrote Gandhi, "for I know that God is neither in heaven, nor down below, but in every one."[5]

Gandhi and Andrews remained rooted in their respective religious traditions, but the quality of religious seeking inspired them to cross boundaries. They recognized that the Truth they sought was greater than the traditions to which they belonged and they sought to learn from each other. They were united also in the conviction that the God they served lived in all beings and in creation, and that love for God must find expression in life as a servant. Gandhi gave his friend the affectionate title *dinabandhu* (friend of the poor). A deep yearning for God and a commitment to the poor and oppressed drew them to each other and provided the common ground for their friendship. Gandhi and Andrews shared a deep value for the common humanity of the poor and this was inseparable from the discernment of their own shared humanity as seekers after God. Gandhi and Andrews discovered their common humanity and shared identity by recognizing in one another the earnest seeker and the servant of the poor. Where do we today find our common ground with persons of other traditions?

Ethical Obligations

The ethical dimension of interreligious friendships is perhaps its most difficult and challenging, but it is also the one that saves such a relationship from superficiality and relativism. It reminds us that interreligious friendships do not require that we dispose of our deepest values and the theological commitments that serve as our norms for decision-making. The nature and sources of our ethical criteria must be explicitly articulated and we cannot entirely avoid conversations about justice/injustice, oppression/liberation, and caste/racism. Interreligious friendships allow us to be questioned and to question, our practice and understanding of ethical obligations. Friendship is deepened when it permits such mutual questioning and opens up the possibility for ethical growth and transformation.

The growth and maturity of an interreligious friendship into one in which each enjoys the liberty to critically question and disagree with the other is powerfully exemplified in the Gandhi–Andrews relationship. Gandhi expected his Christian friends to be critical of him. In a letter to Horace Alexander, a friend and colleague of Gandhi and Andrews, Gandhi implored him to "criticize me as frankly and fearlessly as Charlie used to do."[6] He concluded a letter to Andrews, one in which he disagreed with Andrews, with the following words.

> Instead of a letter, I have inflicted upon you what may almost read like an essay. But it was necessary that you should know what is passing in my mind at the present moment. You may now pronounce your

> judgement and mercilessly tear my ideas to pieces where you find them to be wrong.[7]

Andrews and Gandhi disagreed publicly on several significant issues. Andrews was opposed to Gandhi's vow of celibacy. He did not think it should be prescribed for everyone joining the *ashram* community. For Gandhi, it was essential to his life of religious seeking and his commitment to the service of India. Andrews felt that Gandhi's efforts to enlist Indians to fight on behalf of the Allied cause in the First World War betrayed his emphasis on nonviolence as a moral force. Gandhi, in his turn, argued that one who lacked the ability to use force, cannot claim to be nonviolent. Andrews argued with Gandhi about his tactic of setting fire to imported clothing, claiming that it created the conditions for violence. Gandhi saw it as a necessary part of his emphasis on using locally made cloth and developing economic self-sufficiency. Gandhi's response to Andrews's stinging criticism speaks to the trust established between them. "It is so like him," wrote Gandhi. "Whenever he feels hurt over anything I have done–and this is by no means the first of such occasions–he deluges me with letters without waiting for an answer. *For it is love speaking to love, not arguing.* And so it has been over the burning of foreign clothes."[8] Their profound loving friendship enabled them to be critical of each other's choices and saved their relationship from dogmatism and superficiality. A secure interreligious friendship that allows such critical interrogation is rare and such rarity points to one of the challenges. It certainly requires humility and, in the case of Gandhi and Andrews, a sense that the journey to God is an ongoing process. They were influential leaders but deeply conscious of their limits as human beings. How do we develop interreligious relationships that allow mutual, ethical questioning?

Mutual Trust

Tulasidasa's explication of mutual trust as implying that one speaks in public only about the virtues of the other is significant for interreligious friendship. It makes us aware of our proclivity to speak of our own traditions in the ideal, to ignore the gulf between ideal and reality, but to speak loudly about the *realities* of other traditions. The historical realities of all our traditions, however, leave much to be desired. In his concluding address to the World's Parliament of Religions (September 27, 1893), Swami Vivekananda reminded his listeners that the interreligious gathering proved that "holiness, purity, and charity are not the exclusive possessions of any church in the world, and that every system has produced men and women of the most exalted character."

In interreligious friendships, we grow in appreciation of the complexity of other traditions and understand their deepest aspirations. We are careful in our public utterances about persons of other traditions, extending to them the same charitable considerations that we wish extended to us. The face of our friend is always before us and we learn to speak the same in absence as in his presence. When trust is not established, public criticism of another tradition will be heard as demonization.

Gandhi seems to interpret the meaning of mutual trust in interreligious relationships in a manner different from Tulasidasa. Gandhi does not rule out public criticism of other traditions and of his own tradition, but he believed that the right to criticize another tradition had to be earned. One had to first befriend the other, and to show reverence for all that is good in the other tradition. In one of his well-known statements, Gandhi spoke of the "duty of every cultured man or woman to read sympathetically the scriptures of the world. If we are to respect others' religions, as we would have them respect our own, a friendly study of the world's religions is a sacred duty."[9] One should seek understanding of other traditions by pondering the writings of those who are practitioners of those traditions.

> There is one rule which should always be kept in mind while studying all great religions, and that is that one should study them only through the writings of votaries of the respective religions. For instance, if one wants to study the Bhagavat, one should do so not through a translation of it made by a hostile critic, but one prepared by a lover of the Bhagavat.[10]

Gandhi was writing these words at a time when, other than Hindu practitioners, missionaries with a proselytizing agenda produced most of the studies on the tradition. Today, we have a vast body of work from scholars who do not share this agenda and that are very useful for our understanding of the tradition. But Gandhi's point is valid. The voices of those who live the tradition must inform significantly our understanding.

Andrews earned the trust and friendship of Gandhi and Hindus by his earnest efforts to understand the tradition and to enter into its spirit. He felt that it was his Christian obligation to search out the wisdom of Hinduism and he sought to share with fellow Christians its spiritual richness. At the same time, Andrews was well aware of the oppressive practices and structures that were present in Hindu society and he was outspoken about these. He cooperated closely with Gandhi for the removal of untouchability. He commended the work of reform movements within Hinduism such as the Arya Samaj and Brahmo Samaj.

Andrews spoke strongly against Christian missionaries who emphasized only the historical flaws of the tradition and not its spiritual riches. He repudiated a British author who wrote of Hinduism as a disease.

> Those of us who have lived among the Hindus and have witnessed the deep sincerity of their religious life, especially that of the women in the household, can do nothing but writhe at the insults which she pours upon the Hindu faith as though it were one of the most obscene things on earth. Her object seems to be to exalt the special virtues of the British. She tries to do this in such a way as to afford to a certain type of Englishman or women a secret satisfaction at the contrast with his own ideals and make him say within himself, like the Pharisee of old: "God I thank Thee that I am not as the other men are, or even as this Hindu."[11]

Andrews and Gandhi crossed what Diana Eck refers to as the "terra incognita on the map of interreligious dialogue."[12] Their friendship and trust created a safe space for mutual questioning and criticism. In fact, Andrews is a truly remarkable example of a Christian who was embraced as a friend by Hindus and whose criticism was understood as springing from an unambiguous love for Hindu and Hinduism. His friendship was transparent. Gandhi and Hindus did not suspect a hidden agenda.

Generosity

Generosity is the mutuality of giving and receiving. Interreligious friendships cannot grow and flourish if one thinks of oneself as having everything to give and nothing to receive. The generosity of giving must be complemented by the humility and openness of receiving. It seems difficult to enter into deep friendship with someone of another tradition, whose theological conclusions permitted only a one-way conversation and whose relationship is determined a priori by theological positions and not by encounters with practitioners. Andrews saw clearly that Christian missionaries went out to India only to give, without any thought of receiving. They sought the worst in the tradition and not the best. On his part, Andrews entered the world of Hinduism not blindly, but as a reverential seeker, and he imbibed deeply from its nourishing spirituality.

Andrews's religious life was deepened and enriched by his study of Hinduism and his friendship with Gandhi. His understanding of God, prior to this encounter, emphasized the nature of God as creator and ruler, existing outside of creation and inviting awe. "But when I went deep into the heart of India," wrote Andrews, "I found the whole emphasis to be laid on the realization of God inwardly and spiritually within the soul. There was no less awe than in the west, but it was more of an inward character. This, when fully grasped, brought me nearer to Saint John's gospel than the ordinary western teaching. It meant that not only Christ could say, 'I and my Father are one,' but that we, as God's children, in all reverence, could say this also."[13] His friendship with the Hindu tradition opened new windows of understanding into his own. Gandhi's own deep learning from Christianity is well-known. He was moved by the Sermon on the Mount and he described Jesus as the "Prince of *satyagrahis*." It was the Sermon on the Mount, he claimed, that truly awoke him to the value of nonviolent resistance. He acknowledged the influence of Jesus on him and commended him, in remarkable words, to other Hindus.

> Jesus occupies in my heart the place of one of the greatest teachers who have made a considerable influence on my life. Leave the Christians alone for the present. I shall say to the Hindus that your lives will be incomplete unless you reverently study the teachings of Jesus.[14]

Gandhi's openness to entering into friendships with persons of other faiths was the expression of his desire, as he famously put it, not to live in a house "walled in on all sides and my windows and doors to be stuffed. I want the cultures of all lands to be blown about my house as freely as possible. Mine is not a religion of the prison-house."

There is no doubt that Gandhi's friendship with Andrews deepened his appreciation for Christianity. He spoke of Andrews as a *rishi* (holy teacher), one of the highest Hindu titles conferred upon a human being. He used the example of his friend to implore Indians not to hate the British. "As long as there is even one Andrews among the British people," wrote Gandhi, "we must, for the sake of such as one, bear no hatred to them."

The Risks of Friendship

Interreligious friendships, as the relationship between Gandhi and Andrews demonstrates, are not without risks. In the case of Gandhi, he had to deal with the accusation that his friend's influence on him was too strong, especially in the matter of advocating on behalf of the untouchables. Gandhi's sensitivity to this criticism could be discerned easily in a letter he wrote to Andrews in response to Andrews's prodding that he makes this work his central purpose in life.

> You are thinking as an Englishman. I must not keep one thing from you. The *Gujarati* is endeavoring to weaken my proposition on the question by saying that I have been influenced by you in this matter, meaning thereby that I am not speaking as a Hindu but as one having been spoiled by being under your Christian influence. This is all rotten,

> I know. I began this work in South Africa before I ever heard of you and I was conscious of the sin of untouchability before I came under other Christian influences in South Africa.[15]

On Andrews's side, he had to deal with the condemnation of the white South Africans for his friendship with Gandhi and, on one occasion, bending to touch Gandhi's feet. He faced opposition because of his association with the Arya Samaj, a reformist Hindu movement that was opposed to Christian proselytization. Fellow Christians questioned his commitment and loyalty to Christianity.

Underlying the accusations directed at Gandhi and Andrews, is the fear that such deep friendships across traditions will diminish one's commitment and faithfulness to one's own tradition. Gandhi was very well aware of this fear and spoke to it.

> Let no one, even for a moment, entertain the fear that a reverent study of other religions is likely to weaken or shake one's faith in one's own.[16]

It is not that Gandhi held the Hindu tradition to be perfect. Far from such a view, he professed that his religion bore all the marks of human imperfection. He likened his relationship with Hinduism to his relationship with his wife, who moves him, despite her faults, like no other woman does. With her, he shares an indissoluble bond.

Division on Conversion

On the matter of conversion, one of the most contentious issues between Hindus and Christians in India, these two friends remained divided. Andrews was certainly not a missionary in the traditional sense. He repudiated conversion programs and material rewards to induce conversion. He shared with Gandhi a belief that one's life speaks for one's tradition more than words or preaching. Gandhi appreciated that attempts to convert him to Christianity never intruded on their friendship. He made special mention of this quality of their relationship in an address to Christian missionaries.

> If I want a pattern on the ideal missionary, I should instance C.F. Andrews. If he were here, he would blush for what I want to say. I believe that he is today truer, broader, and better for his toleration of the other principal religions of the world. He never speaks with me about conversion to Christianity though we are closest friends. I have many friends, but the friendship between Charlie Andrews and myself is especially deep.[17]

Yet, unlike Gandhi, Andrews believed that conversion from one tradition to another should be possible. It meant for him the seeking of baptism in the Christian church, following an inner spiritual experience.

> If conversion meant the denial of any living truth in one's own religion, then we must have nothing to do with it. But it is rather the discovery of a new and glorious truth for which one would sacrifice one's life. It does mean also, very often, passing from one fellowship to another and this should never be done lightly.[18]

Gandhi has commented extensively on the matter of conversion and his view must be seen in the context of colonial India, where the Christian tradition was an ally of the exploitative British Empire. In general, he was opposed to all conversion. A person, in Gandhi's views, should adhere to his religion, not because he considers it to be the best among all religions, but because he can transform it by learning from other traditions and help it to grow towards a fuller understanding of truth by the enrichment of other traditions. This is the substance of his famous lines.

> So, we can pray, if we are Hindus, not that a Christian should become a Hindu; or if we are Mussalmans, not that a Hindu or Christian should become a Mussalman; nor should we even secretly pray that anyone should be converted; but our inmost prayer should be that a Hindu should be a better Hindu, a Muslim a better Muslim and a Christian a better Christian.[19]

It is clear that any obsessive and persistent efforts to convert the other in a relationship of interreligious friendship would not have Gandhi's approval. At the same time, he welcomed the influence that friends of different traditions have on each other through the power of their traditions in their lives. He compared this often to the fragrance of a rose.

> The rose irresistibly draws people to itself and the scent remains with them. Even so, the aroma of Christianity is subtler even than that of the rose and should, therefore, be imparted in an even quieter, and more imperceptible manner, if possible.[20]
>
> Faith is not imparted like secular subjects. It is given through the language of the heart. If a man has a living faith in him, it spreads its aroma like a rose its scent. Because of its invisibility, the extent of its influence is far wider than that of the visible beauty of the colour of the petals.[21]

Friendship is the relationship that allows us to breathe in the fragrance of each other's religious lives.

Some Practical Suggestions

- Interreligious friendships are not possible without the existence of religious differences. An attitude to other religions that problematizes the fact of religious difference and devotes itself to the ideal of homogenization is not conducive to the formation of interreligious friendships. We need to promote a culture that values commitment to faith traditions while promoting the sharing of wisdom across traditions and a value and respect for religious diversity. Diversity is not a problem to be overcome and our discourse about religious diversity should never be framed in these terms.

- The deep meaning and value of human friendship is exploited and trivialized when it is employed as a part of a strategic plan to proselytize and win converts. Such instrumentalization of friendship causes mistrust and suspicion, and leads to the construction of defensive barriers. Friendship should not be used as a ploy in a program of conversion.

- Friendship is meaningful when the relationship is informed by a willingness to receive and to give, to teach and to be taught. The mutuality of giving and receiving in friendship is possible only when friends are willing to profess their distinctive understandings of truth, but to admit also that truth exceeds all finite human formulations and expressions. We need, like Mahatma Gandhi and Charles Andrews, to recognize that truth is not limited by the boundaries of our traditions and may be discovered in deeper ways through friendships with persons of other religions.

- The understanding of our neighbors of other faiths is an important need in our contemporary context of life in religiously diverse communities. The religious traditions of our neighbors are embodied in their lives and entering into friendships with them deepens our understanding of their tradition and what it means to them. Opportunities and spaces for such friendships must be welcomed and encouraged.

- Interreligious friendships must not mean that we conceal our core theological commitments and values. Mature friendships allow us to question and to be questioned, avoiding superficiality and dogmatism. This is the ideal that we recommend, but recognize that such a relationship requires profound trust that is not always immediate. Like all other meaningful relationships, interreligious friendships require effort and commitment, and their demands must not be underestimated. The models that we recommend should reflect the honesty of mutual questioning and criticism.

- Theological learning and sharing nourish interreligious friendships. These relationships also grower stronger and more meaningful through shared commitments to justice and the service of the oppressed and disadvantaged. Such commitments give meaning to friendship and are especially important in the context of our shared communities.

- Although the theological barriers to interreligious friendships are lower in the Hindu tradition, there are other barriers. Caste and Hindu nationalist ideology that devalue and marginalize others are examples of such problems. Our discussion of theological issues cannot be separate from the social and political realities that also affect human relationships across traditions.

Concluding Thoughts

Gandhi and Andrews shared a rare and remarkable friendship. They recognized in each other a deep yearning for God and a commitment to the service of the suffering. The love, trust, sharing, and critical questioning that their relationship exemplified are vital for understanding meaningful relations across religious frontiers and instructive as we ponder the challenges of such relationships.

I started this essay by noting that friendship, in the Hindu worldview, is the ideal towards which we must aspire in all relationships. A person who realizes the ideal of friendship overcomes the dualism of "friend" and "enemy," and sees all beings with the vision of friendship. Gandhi reached for this ideal in his relationships even with those against whom he struggled. It is well-known that he made a pair of sandals for General Jan Smuts who imprisoned him in South Africa. He wrote polite letters to his adversaries, including Lord Irwin, the Viceroy of India, and signed such letters with the words, "Your friend, M.K. Gandhi."

Interreligious friendship is a particular expression of this universal ideal of friendship between human beings. It is made possible, however, by the more general ideal of friendship that enables us, in the first instance, to reach out to human beings across constructed boundaries. As a particular relationship, it has its own potential and challenges. As Gandhi and Andrews helps us to see so powerfully, religious difference is not, in and of itself, a barrier to such relationships. They remind us that such friendships do not occur between traditions, but between human beings with different visions of truth.

The challenge of mutual understanding is no small one, but is made possible when such relationships are nourished in the fertile soil of mutual trust, identity with the other, compassion, generosity, and freedom to question and be questioned. There are, as we have seen, risks in such friendship, but the Gandhi–Andrews relationship is a resounding "yes" to interreligious friendship and an invitation to share its rich possibilities. I conclude with the words of Charles Andrews summing up what his friend meant to him.

> Our hearts met from the first moment we saw one another and they have remained united by the strongest ties of love ever since. To be with him was an inspiration which awakened all that was best in me and gave me a high courage, enkindled and enlightened by his own.[22]

References

1 Cited in David McI Gracie, ed., *Gandhi and Charlie: The Story of a Friendship* (Massachusetts: Cowley Publications, 1989), 41.

2 Cited in K.L. Seshagiri Rao, *Mahatma Gandhi and C.F. Andrews* (Patiala: Punjabi University, 1969), 11.

3 Mahatma Gandhi, *All Men Are Brothers* (New York: Continuum, 2001), 61.

4 Rao, *Mahatma Gandhi and C.F. Andrews*, 64.

5 Gandhi, *All Men Are Brothers, 34.*

6 Gracie, *Gandhi and Charlie*, 3.

7 Gracie, *Gandhi and Charlie*, 61.

8 Gracie, *Gandhi and Charlie*, 97-98.

9 Shriman Narayan, *The Voice of Truth* (Ahmedabad: The Navajivan Trust, 1969), 267.

10 M. K Gandhi, *All Religions are True*, ed. A. T. Hingorani (Mumbai: Bharatiya Vidya Bhavan, 1962), 231.

11 Cited in Rao, *Mahatma Gandhi and C.F. Andrews*, 44.

12 Eck, *Encountering God*, 223.

13 Gracie, *Gandhi and Charlie*, 19-20.

14 M. K. Gandhi, *The Message of Jesus Christ (*Bombay: Bharatiya Vidya Bhavan, 1963), 42.

15 Gracie, *Gandhi and Charlie,*138.

16 Gandhi, *All Religions Are True*, 22.

17 Gandhi, *All Religions Are True*, 175.

18 Rao, *Mahatma Gandhi and C. F. Andrews*, 54.

19 Gandhi, *The Message of Jesus Christ*, 52.

20 Gandhi, *The Message of Jesus Christ*, 63

21 Gandhi, *The Message of Jesus Christ*, 61

22 C.F. Andrews, *What I Owe to Christ* (New York: Abingdgon Press, 1932), 222-23.

PART III

LIBERATION

CHAPTER EIGHT

THE RESOURCES AND CHALLENGES FOR A HINDU THEOLOGY OF LIBERATION

Liberation Theology

Liberation theology, described by Deane William Ferm as, "the major Christian theological achievement of the twentieth century," was inspired significantly by the deliberations of the Second Vatican Council (1962–65), especially by its summon to eliminate economic inequalities.[1] Consistent with the prophetic tradition of Judaism, the distinguishing tenet of liberation theology is "a preferential option for the poor," expressed passionately in a religiously motivated commitment to liberate the oppressed from injustice and suffering. This commitment is articulated in a comprehensive understanding of the meaning of liberation, that shifts the emphasis from postmortem existence to the quality of existence in this life. Liberation is no longer narrowly construed as emancipation from suffering in a future life. Its meaning is centered also on freedom from poverty, powerlessness, and injustice in this life and world.

In contrast to the traditional emphasis on the personal and individual nature of evil, liberation theologians call attention to evil as a social phenomenon. While recognizing the significance of personal choice and responsibility, the focus is upon "systemic evil," that is the suffering that human beings inflict upon each other by unjust economic, social, and political systems. Liberation theologians call attention to the social character of human existence and to the ways in which injustice is embedded in the conventional structures of society. The apartheid system of South Africa, for example, was not merely an expression of personal race prejudice. It was legitimized by law and Biblical interpretations, and embodied in social, economic and political systems. The implication of this emphasis is that genuine change will be achieved only through the change and transformation of such systems. The reform of individual lives will not, by itself, result in the comprehensive liberation from structural oppression.

"Structural injustice," as Maguire puts it, "requires structural relief and a relativizing of private claims by setting them in their social context."[2]

For the liberation theologian, spirituality and justice are inseparable. The practice of justice in human relationships is the highest social expression of the religious life. The interior life of holiness and piety must find outward expression in a commitment to justice. These two dimensions of authentic spirituality mutually nourish and are incomplete without each other. Without the concern for justice, personal piety becomes obsessively self-centered. At the same time, attentiveness to and cultivation of the interior spiritual life nourishes and provides the motivation for the work of justice. Justice, it must be emphasized, cannot be equated with charity. The latter seeks to offer relief and care to those who are the victims of injustice. Justice seeks to change and transform the structures that cause suffering. "Charity means helping the victims. Justice asks, 'Why are there so many victims?' and then seeks to change the causes of victimization, that is, the way the system is structured."[3] One of the distinguishing marks of liberation theology is that its commitment to economic, political and social freedom is rooted in a religious worldview in which the understanding of what it means to be human is derived from a vision of the nature of God.

In the case of the Christian tradition, a significant impetus to liberation theology, as noted, came from the deliberations of the second Vatican Council (1962–65) and especially by its call to eliminate poverty. In the tradition of Buddhism, the engaged Buddhist movement, associated with the thought and life of the Vietnamese Zen Buddhist teacher, Thich Nhat Hanh, articulates similar concerns. The concern among engaged Buddhists is to apply the wisdom and practices of the Buddhist tradition, to overcome suffering caused by injustice and oppression in the socio-political and economic spheres.[4] In the case of the Hindu tradition, there is no organized movement corresponding to the engaged Buddhist movement, or to Christian liberation theology. There are individual Hindu leaders and interpreters who have articulated the significance of religion for social change. On the whole, liberation theology has received scant attention from contemporary Hindu commentators and thinkers, and there is a clear need for the articulation of a comprehensive understanding of liberation rooted in the Hindu tradition.

In this chapter, I argue for the necessity of such a theology and identify the theological resources within the tradition that may be summoned in its support. It is essential for the development of a theology of liberation that scholars and practitioners be ready and willing to acknowledge the reality of injustice, past and present, in our traditions. We need to be more self-critical and less defensive. Citing the injustices of other traditions does not justify or excuse those within our own. There are many, in India and elsewhere, who address issues of injustice from outside the Hindu tradition. I do so as a committed insider, as an engaged lover of my tradition.

The Need for a Hindu Theology of Liberation

The necessity for a Hindu liberation tradition arises from the fact that, as in other religious traditions, there are issues of injustice that need to be addressed. Prominent among these are caste and patriarchy. It is unfortunate that in both of these areas, the argument and struggle for justice are too often disconnected from the Hindu tradition. In the case of caste oppression, many seek liberation, not through engagement with Hinduism, but by conversion to other religions or even by the rejection of religion. It is instructive that the largest number of converts in India from Hindu traditions to Buddhism, Christianity and Islam, come from the so-called untouchable castes, popularly referred to as the Dalits. The most famous convert, Dr. B. R. Ambedkar, felt hopeless about the possibility of social liberation through Hinduism, publicly renounced the tradition and, with almost three million followers, embraced Buddhism. He was convinced that caste injustice and oppression were intrinsic to Hinduism.[5] It is urgent therefore, that we ask whether the Hindu tradition offers a justification for concern about injustice in the world and resources for addressing these.

Hinduism, like other world religions that developed in patriarchal cultures, reflects assumptions about male gender supremacy that have caused suffering to women. Gender injustice manifests itself in the fact that a disproportionate percentage of the illiterate in India are women, and in the abortion of female fetuses because of a preference for male offspring. It manifests also in the stigmatization of widows, and in the custom of dowry that depletes the economic resources of families into which girls are born and that makes them feel guilty for being women. According to the 2011 population census in India, the sex ratio, though improving, is 940 females for every 1,000 males.[6] In many traditions, women were excluded from the study of sacred texts and represented as incapable of attaining liberation.

The necessity for a Hindu theology of liberation, however, should not be made only on the basis of various forms of injustice within Hindu society. India itself is a multireligious society and Hindus live in many parts of our world in plural communities, challenged by problems of poverty and all its associated problems, that include lack of health care, employment, adequate wages, opportunities for education, and poor or inadequate housing. In the interreligious and interrelated context of our lives today, we are challenged to respond to human problems and needs beyond the boundaries of our traditions. Liberation theologies are needed for the pursuit of the universal common good.

Challenges to the Development of a Hindu Theology of Liberation

What are the challenges to the development of a Hindu theology of liberation? Keeping in mind the concern of liberation theology with the overcoming of suffering and injustice in this life, there are six challenges that I wish to identify.

First, liberation theology requires that we take life in this world seriously. We may not attribute the highest value to the world, but this is not the same as promoting indifference to the world and the conditions of human life. There are prominent interpretations of the world in the Hindu tradition that liken it to an illusion of the senses, that we conjure and experience because of our ignorance of true reality. When true reality is known, the world recedes in significance and meaning. The prominent Hindu philosopher T.M. P. Mahadevan puts it this way,

> Just as things and events seen in a dream vanish altogether and become meaningless when one wakes up, so does the universe with all its contents disappear when one finds the Real Self. One then becomes perfectly awakened to what really exists, the Absolute. Compared with That, the universe is no more than a dream. So long as one sees in a dream, the dream objects are intensely real. So also is the universe with all its contents to one under the spell of *avidyā* (ignorance). *On awakening to Absolute Reality, however, all these have no value, no meaning, no existence.*[7]

If the reality of the world is underplayed in this manner, it is not consistent for one to be affected by events within it. To respond to the world is to grant reality to the world; it is to treat as real that which does not, in reality, exist. Interpretations like these provide justification for world-renunciation. Taken to their extremes, these interpretations make it difficult to take the issues of the world, such as poverty and injustice, seriously. The world is represented as beset with problems and one is advised to cultivate an attitude of disgust towards it, and pray to be free from its clutches. The negativization of the world promotes indifference and a wish to escape life.

Second, and connected with the first, are the interpretations of the meaning of liberation (*mokṣa*) that equate it entirely with freedom from the world and from the cycle of birth, death and rebirth, referred to as *saṁsāra*. *Saṁsāra* is a term with negative connotations. It is equated with ignorance and suffering. When the world itself is equated with *saṁsāra*, the focus is on attaining freedom from the world and not on solving its problems.

> Since, the process of the births and rebirths is so beset with troubles, therefore, one should cultivate a feeling of disgust. That is because it is found that wretched creatures are, every moment of their lives, taken up by the pangs of births and deaths and are thrust into illimitable, terrible darkness—like the unnavigable ocean, and having no hope of getting out. Therefore one should cultivate feelings of disgust towards this process of birth and rebirth—avoid it, shun it, praying "May I never fall into this terrible metempsychic ocean."[8]

Third, are those interpretations of the doctrine of *karma* that comprehensively seek to explain all events in the present life as having causes that may be traced to actions performed earlier in this life or in previous lives. Such rigid interpretations of *karma* dispose us to seeing all forms of suffering, even injustice and oppression, as deserved and explicable by actions in the past. In this worldview, there is no injustice. The victim is responsible for his suffering and not the particular social or economic system that prevails. The perception of suffering as justified, undermines the motivation to struggle for change. The writer D.C. Sharma, for example, attributes inequality to *karma*.

> On no other hypothesis, can we explain the inequalities of life that we see all around us. God is not partial. He would not of his own accord make one man strong and another weak, one man healthy and another man sickly, and one man sensual and another man spiritual. He would never of his own accord put one man in surroundings that help the progress of his soul and another man in surroundings that hinder his progress. The inequalities of life are due to ourselves and not to God. We carry our own past.[9]

The relationship between systemic structures of injustice and inequality are not considered in this perspective. Birth into an unjust social order is seen as the consequence of *karma* and thus deserved.

Fourth, these interpretations of *karma* have also been deployed by many to argue for the hierarchical social order of caste; in this worldview, one is born into a caste and into all the socio-economic and cultural factors obtaining. Freedom from any caste is possible only by rebirth. Swami Viditatmananda, for example, although making an argument for caste divisions based on inner disposition and not birth, argues that in the absence of a method of measuring disposition, birth is an objective criterion of caste.

> The principle of the law of *karma* is involved in this determination. A person is born in a given family, in a given environment in keeping with his past *karma*. The situation will be appropriate to work out his *karma*. A *śūdra* is born as that because that is the appropriate place according to his *karma* and he will have the disposition of a *śūdra*. Since we do not have a way to judge the inner disposition because it is subjective, an objective criterion has to be accepted.[10]

Instead of arguing about the validity of particular criteria, we must make arguments for the overcoming of all caste divisions. Caste is a complex social system that intersects with all dimensions of the lives of those whose identities are formed and defined by its categories and its hierarchical ordering of human beings. The value that it confers on those in its upper ranks is in relation to the devaluing of those who are regarded as lower. Devaluation leads to the perception of people as objects and not as fellow beings who feel and suffer like us. It provides the conditions for guilt-free violence and mistreatment.

Fifth, is the fact that the major commentators of sacred texts, past and present, are renouncers who entered the fourth stage of Hindu life (*saṁnyāsa*). With rare exceptions, the renouncer had minimal interest in the matters of the world. The renouncer entered a state of existence comparable to one who has died. The identity of the renouncer is no longer connected with family or community; this is signified by the assumption of a new name. One of the consequences of renunciation is social death; one's responsibility for the fulfillment of mutual obligations to family and community comes to an end. The renouncer is exempt from having to perform traditional religious rituals. Entering into the fourth stage of life also frees the renouncer from having to fulfill obligations that are associated with what we regard as work or profession. Freedom from ritual and professional obligations becomes possible because the consequences that ensue from renunciation are similar to those that follow the death of an individual. As Patrick Olivelle notes, renunciation results in the dissolution of marriage, freedom from contractual debts, and the distribution of property among heirs.[11] Free from social ties and identities, it should not surprise that renouncers demonstrated little interest in social justice in their commentaries and teachings.

Sixth, is the rise and dominance of the ideology of Hindu nationalism or Hindutva. Hindutva, as I employ the term here, is an interpretation of the meaning of Hindu identity advocated by Vinayak

Damodar Savarkar (1883–1966).[12] Savarkar's definition of Hindu identity has several important components. The first is geographical. A Hindu is "primarily a citizen, either in himself or through his forefathers of 'Hindusthan.'" There is common blood or *jāti*. A Hindu is a descendant of Hindu parents, and shares with other Hindus a common blood, traceable to the Vedic fathers. "We *feel* we are a JATI, a race bound together by the dearest ties of blood and therefore it must be so."[13] The third is the tie of homage to Hindu culture or civilization. Savarkar names this common culture as Sanskriti, on the basis of the claim that Sanskrit is the language that expresses and preserves all that is worthy in the history of the Hindus. It includes a shared history, literature, art, law, festivals, rites, rituals and heroes. This criterion was the basis for the exclusion, not only of Indian Muslims, but also of Indian Christians. Despite sharing birth and blood, they had, in Savarkar's words, "ceased to own Hindu civilization (Sanskriti) as a whole. They belong, or feel that they belong, to a cultural unit altogether different from the Hindu one."[14] A Hindu, according to Savarkar, is someone who looks upon India as not only fatherland, but also as holy land.

Savarkar's narrow identification of Hindu identity with birth, blood and common culture, minimizes the significance of theology and the possibilities for the tradition to transcend ties of nationality and ethnicity. It confers a quasi-divine status to the nation and proposes the highest aim of life to be the service and defense of the fatherland. It is a definition of the meaning of Hindu identity based on exclusion and otherness. It considerably narrows the concerns of the tradition and gives no value or emphasis to the tradition having anything to do with the overcoming of suffering and injustice. It is hostile to self-critical analysis of tradition. It does not speak to universal human concerns or problematize structures of injustice. Its dominance in the contemporary Hindu world is a matter of deep concern.

What are the resources within the Hindu tradition for a theology of liberation? Is it possible to articulate a world affirming theology that enables us to contest the devaluation of the world and indifference to the concerns of life in the world? I believe that there are alternative interpretations of the tradition that affirm a greater value for the world, and offer a vision of a liberated life that puts the emphasis on a transformed way of being and new relationships here and now. In what follows, I identify some of these resources. I do so by identifying the requirements for a Hindu theology of liberation, and then highlighting the relevant resources in texts and interpretations.

Requirements and Resources for a Hindu Theology of Liberation

First, a Hindu liberation theology requires a value for the world ontologically.

The *Upaniṣads*, or the wisdom section of the Vedas, speak of the absolute (*brahman*) as "That from which all beings originate, by which they are sustained and to which they return (*Taittirīya Upaniṣad* 3.1.1). Other *Upaniṣads* (e.g. *Chāndogya Upaniṣad* 6.2.1-2) speak of *brahman* as the indivisible and uncreated One from which the many are created. The *Upaniṣads* contest the existence of anything but the One before creation, and the emergence of the world from anything other than this One. The universe, *Chāndogya Upaniṣad* emphatically states, does not spontaneously appear from non-existence.

Advaita, the ancient and influential Hindu nondual theological tradition, speaks of the relationship between *brahman* and the world as not-two. It does not equate the world pantheistically with God, but does not also grant the world an ontological existence independent of God. The world does not have to exist independently of *brahman* to have value. This argument implies that only theologies of dualism can confer value to the world. On the contrary, since *brahman* has ultimate value, the non-dual relationship enriches the value of the world. The Hindu tradition offers us resources for seeing the world as *brahman's* marvelous outpouring and as a celebrative expression of its fullness. Its value is derived from the fact that it originates from, exists in, and shares the nature of *brahman*, even though, as a finite process, it can never fully express *brahman*. If the world is seen positively as the outcome of the intentional creativity of *brahman*, expressing and sharing the fullness of *brahman*, the world does not have to be rejected or devalued. I contest those interpretations cited earlier, that equate the reality of the world to a dream or illusion.[15]

Second, a Hindu liberation theology requires an understanding of the meaning liberation (mokṣa) that values life in this world and not escape from the world.

A world affirming theology of creation enables us to contest interpretations that problematize and devalue the world itself and equate liberation with freedom from the world. Challenging such interpretations allows us to emphasize that the human problem is not the world or human existence itself, but that which Hindu traditions, in their different ways, speak of as *avidyā* or a deep and consequential ignorance, about the nature of reality and, especially, the Self. In the condition of ignorance, we regard the human self as distinct and separate from all other selves and the world of nature. At the heart of *avidyā* is an ontological misunderstanding. Liberation, first and foremost, is freedom from this misunderstanding or false knowledge. *Moksa*, therefore, is not freedom from the world, but an awakening to and a transformation into a new way of being in the world.

There are numerous texts in the Hindu tradition emphasizing that, for the liberated, the world does not disappear as an illusion does, when right knowledge dawns. It is seen in a new relationship to its source and ground. Typical of such texts are the following from the *Bhagavadgītā* (13:28;18;20): "One who sees the great Lord existing equally in all beings, the imperishable in the perishable, truly sees" ; "That knowledge by which one sees one imperishable being in all beings, indivisible in the divisible, is the highest." *Īśā Upaniṣad* (1) begins with the beautiful text: "All this–whatsoever moves on the earth–should be covered with God (*īśā vāsyam idam sarvam yat kiñca jagatyām jagat*)."

The world exists both for the one who knows and for the one who does not know. The difference is that the knower of *brahman* understands the world in its right relationship to *brahman*. The eyes of the liberated are not closed to the world, but fully open and seeing it in a transformed way. Several Hindu traditions attest to the possibility of what is referred to as living liberation (*jīvanmukti*), attesting to the compatibility of liberation with life in the world.

Third, a Hindu theology of liberation requires detailing the ethical implications and obligations of mokṣa for the transformation of human relationships and social structures.

Why is this important? Traditionally, liberation is sought through entry into the fourth stage of life, the stage of renunciation (*saṁnyāsa*). This stage, as noted earlier, is comparable to one who is dead. Responsibility for the fulfillment of mutual obligations with family and community comes to an end. The renouncer is exempt also from having to perform traditional rituals. Entering into the fourth stage of life also frees the renouncer from having to fulfill obligations associated with what we regard as work. Renunciation results in the dissolution of marriage, freedom from contractual debts, and the distribution of property among heirs. The consequence of this understanding of renunciation and its relationship to liberation is minimal; there is no interest in speaking about or working out the implications of liberation for life in this world.

As we have seen with our discussion on the status of the world, here also interpretations matter, and the tradition offers resources for alternative and engaged understandings of the ethical implications of liberation. These are interpretations that do not alienate us from the world but draw us into a deeper unity with all.

On two occasions (5:25; 12:4), for example, the *Bhagavadgītā* employs the expression, "delighting in the well-being of all (*sarvabhūtahite ratāḥ*)" to describe the attitude of the liberated in relation to others. The text equates liberation with an empathetic way of being. Liberation makes possible identification with others in suffering and in joy. *Bhagavadgītā* 6:32 praises the best *yogī* as one who knows the pain and joy of others as her own.

The *Bhagavadgītā* (12:13) praises human beings who are without hate, friendly and compassionate (*karuṇa*), nonpossessive, non-ego-centered, tranquil in pleasure and pain, and forgiving. The expression of friendliness (*maitraḥ*) is compassion (*karuṇa*). Later (16:2) compassion towards all (*dayā bhūteṣu*) is listed as the quality of a person enjoying a divine disposition.

These verses, and others, speak of liberation as a new way of being in relation to others and not as the severing of all relationships.

Fourth, a Hindu theology of liberation requires expanding our understanding of suffering and a commitment to working for the overcoming of suffering in its multiple forms.

The traditional emphasis has been on suffering as an inward condition associated with ignorance (*avidyā*) and with freedom from this primary condition, but there is no reason to limit the meaning of suffering in this way. Hindu texts commending the identification with others in suffering do not suggest any such limitation. What we need then is an expansive understanding of both suffering and liberation. There are no good theological reasons why we must ignore the suffering of human beings when they lack opportunities to attain the necessities for dignified and decent living or when suffering is inflicted through oppression and injustice based on gender, birth or race. There is no glorification of involuntary poverty in the Hindu tradition. *Artha* (economic well-being) is one of the four goals of life, along with pleasure (*kāma*), commitment to ethical conduct (*dharma*) and liberation (*mokṣa*). These four goals are referred to, in Sanskrit, as *puruṣārthas*, that is, "human ends." This emphasizes their universality as common ends necessary for the happiness of *all* human beings. These are not, in theory, limited in application by considerations such as gender or caste. It is meaningless, however, to define the good human life as requiring wealth, pleasure, virtue and liberation, and not be concerned about those structures—social, political and economic—that impede and deny persons the opportunities to achieve these ends. A hierarchical social system, like caste or racism, limiting freedom of opportunity and choice, exemplifies such a contradiction. Clearly, it is not enough to articulate common goals; systems that limit people's ability to achieve necessary goals must be identified and changed.

When concern about the overcoming of suffering motivates action in the public sphere, the goal is what the *Bhagavadgītā* (3:20; 3:25) describes as *lokasaṅgraha* or the universal common good. *Loka*, the word that I translate here as "universal," is inclusive. It does not privilege a particular class, profession, gender, ethnic group or species. *Lokasaṅgraha* is a concern for the flourishing of all beings, but must certainly concern itself in a very special way with those who do not flourish because of systemic structures of poverty and injustice. A universal concern must also be attentive to suffering among particular groups in specific contexts. A rarefied concern for all can too easily become a concern for none.

The focus on *avidyā* alone as suffering has resulted in the emphasis on the need for individual cognitive and ethical transformation without attentiveness to the suffering that is inflicted by oppressive social and economic systems and of the need to identify and transform these. My contention is that the Hindu tradition *should* concern itself with such systemic sources of suffering and *does* offer valuable theological resources for addressing and overcoming such suffering.

Fifth, a Hindu theology of liberation requires affirming the equal worth and dignity of all human beings.

The most important teaching in the Hindu tradition for affirming the equal worth and dignity of all human beings is the teaching that the divine exists equally in all beings. Although verses enunciating this insight may be found in various Hindu sacred texts, these are particularly prominent in the *Bhagavadgītā*. *Bhagavadgītā* (13:28-29) provides us with a clear statement.

> One who sees the Supreme God existing equally in all beings, the imperishable in the perishable, truly sees (*samaṁ sarveṣu bhūteṣu tiṣṭhantaṁ parameśvaram vinaśyatsv avinaśyantam yaḥ paśyati sa paśyati*).
>
> Seeing indeed the same God existing everywhere, one does not hurt the self by the self. Therefore, one attains the highest end (*samaṁ paśyan hi sarvatra samavasthitam īśvaram |na hinasty ātmanā 'tmānaṁ tato yāti parāṁ gatim*).

Both verses affirm the presence of God in the world and characterize this presence in two very important ways. The first is by the use of the word *samaṁ*, meaning equally or identically. It is the first word in each of the two verses. The second is *sarveśu bhūteśu*, meaning "in all beings." *Sarvatra* in verse 28 means "everywhere." These words admit to no exclusions nor distinctions. Put simply, the divine exists equally in all beings. The divine presence is not limited by anything—nation, gender, ethnicity, or age. The profound significance that the *Bhagavadgītā* accords to this truth may be appreciated from the fact that its discernment is equated with the attainment of the highest end (*parāṁ gatim*), which is the same as liberation (*mokṣa*).

Racism, sex and age discrimination, and caste are all examples of structures and practices that stand in contradiction to this fundamental teaching on divine immanence. Today, it calls us with urgency to reverence for our common home, the earth, to united efforts to halt its degradation and to promote ecological responsibility in our world.

Two Precursors of Hindu Liberation Theology

Swami Vivekananda

Swami Vivekananda (1863–1902) is the founder of the Ramakrishna Mission and is the most famous disciple of Sri Ramakrishna (1836–1886). He represented Hinduism at the Parliament of World Religions held at Chicago in 1893 and identified himself in a special way with the nondual (Advaita) Hindu tradition.

Vivekananda's motivation for an engaged life of service came in the course of a dialogue with his teacher, Sri Ramakrishna. Speaking to his disciples on one occasion about the meaning of compassion, Ramakrishna explained they should see the service of others as the service of God. "No, no; it is not compassion to *jivas* (living beings) but service to them as Shiva (God)." Swami Vivekananda saw the profound possibilities in this thought for an interpretation of Hinduism that justified service and a concern with overcoming suffering. In memorable words at the Parliament of Religions, Vivekananda told his listeners that, "It is an insult to a starving people to offer them religion; it is an insult to a starving man to teach him metaphysics."[16]

Swami Vivekananda's ontological valuation of the world, from which he derives his justification for an engagement of service, is along the lines argued earlier in this discussion. According to Vivekananda, the value of the world proceeds from its deification. The Hindu tradition, he contends, does not require the denunciation or renunciation of the world; the renunciation required is a relinquishing of a certain interpretation of the significance of the world. Citing the opening verse of *Īśā Upaniṣad*,

Vivekananda says: "Deify it; it is God alone. We read at the commencement of one of the oldest Upaniṣads, 'Whatever exists in this universe is to be covered with the Lord.'"[17] This valuing of the world through its deification is extended also to relationships. One is not called upon to renounce one's family relationships but to see *brahman* in all. Vivekananda criticizes the person whose motivation for activity in the world is greed, but also the person who condemns the world and turns his back on it in favor of ascetic solitude.

> If a man plunges headlong into the foolish luxuries of the world without knowing the truth, he has missed his footing; he cannot reach the goal. And if a man curses the world, goes into a forest, mortifies his flesh, and kills himself little by little by starvation, makes his heart a barren waste, kills out all feelings, and becomes harsh, stern, and dried-up, that man has also missed the way.[18]

In powerful words at the Rameswaram Temple in southern India, Vivekananda called for engaged religion in the service of the poor, the weak, and the diseased. "He who sees Shiva in the poor, in the weak and in the diseased, really worships Shiva; and if he sees Shiva only in the image, his worship is but preliminary."[19]

Swami Vivekananda's deification of the world led logically to a reformulation of the meaning of liberation. This is generally associated in the Hindu tradition with freedom from the cycles of birth, death and rebirth (*saṁsāra*). In a letter to Mary Hale (July 9, 1897), Swami Vivekananda expressed a desire for rebirth and the opportunity it affords for the adoration of God in all.

> May I be born again and again, and suffer thousands of miseries so that I may worship the only God that exists, the only God I believe in, the sum total of all souls—and above all, my God the wicked, my God the miserable, my God the poor of all races, of all species, is the special object of my worship.[20]

What Swami Vivekananda's words make so clear is that, in the Hindu tradition, the human problem is not the fact of birth but ignorance (*avidyā*), because of which the nature of the world's relationship with *brahman* is unrecognized. The deification allows for an embrace of the world and a commitment to the overcoming of suffering.

Mahatma Gandhi

Mahatma Gandhi (1869–1948) described himself as an "Advaitist," but also admitted that his religious views were shaped by a variety of traditions and, in particular, by Jainism and Christianity.

Gandhi described his life's goal as seeing "the universal and all-pervading Spirit of Truth face to face."[21] He sometimes referred to it as the "realization of God." Since this cosmic spirit (*brahman*) was manifested in all beings and did not exist only outside of creation, it can be found only by unity and identity with all beings. The highest expression of this identity, according to Gandhi, is service.

> Man's ultimate aim is the realization of God, and all his activities, social, political, religious, have to be guided by the ultimate aim of the vision of God. The immediate service of all beings becomes a necessary part of the endeavor simply because the only way to find God is to see Him in His creation and to be one with it. This can only be done by the service of all.[22]

Gandhi values the world as a place where one has to opportunity the know the infinite by identifying with, loving, and serving all beings.

Gandhi's activism in the political sphere was also justified by a recourse to a nondual argument. He interpreted Advaita to mean also that all spheres of human activity constituted an indivisible whole. One could not separate the social, political, economic or religious dimensions of human existence into impermeable compartments. All these fields of action are concerned with human well-being. "I could not be leading a religious life," wrote Gandhi, "unless I identified myself with the whole of mankind, and that I could not do unless I took part in politics."[23]

Gandhi foreshadowed one of the defining orientations of liberation theology referred to as the "preferential option for the poor." It is worthwhile to take a careful look at one of the passages in which this preference is described.

> I count no sacrifice too great for the sake of seeing God face to face. The whole of my activity whether it may be called social, political, humanitarian or ethical is directed to that end. And as I know that God is found more often in the lowliest of His creatures than in the high and mighty, I am struggling to reach the status of these. I cannot do so without their service. Hence my passion for the service of the suppressed classes.[24]

This passage reiterates Gandhi's aim in life—of knowing God—and the unity that this goal lends to his multifarious activities. What is new here is his claim that "God is found more often in the lowliest of His creatures than in the high and mighty," and his special commitment to their service. As an *Advaitin*, however, Gandhi's meaning in this passage is not immediately apparent. One of the central tenets of Advaita is the identical existence of *brahman* in all beings, a claim articulated by Gandhi throughout his writings. We may assume then that Gandhi is speaking here about the presence in the poor of those characteristics that we usually associate with those who are cognizant of God. These include virtues such as humility, generosity, compassion, and freedom from greed.

Conclusion

Causing suffering to others and indifference to such suffering are the antithesis of what the Hindu tradition advocates at its highest ethical ideal of nonviolence (*ahiṃsā*). The Hindu tradition offers significant theological resources for the development of a Hindu theology of liberation. The work of developing this theology will not be meaningfully undertaken without attentive listening to the voices of those who experience the tradition as denying them the opportunity and resources to flourish. The tradition must not underplay or explain away the witness of those who experience it as oppressive and unjust, and as denying them power and freedom. Our traditions are challenged in powerful ways by the voices of those at the margins and by those we exclude.

References

1 See Deane William Ferm, "Third World Liberation Theology: Challenge to World Religions," in *World Religions and Human Liberation*, ed. Dan Cohn-Sherbok (Maryknoll: Orbis Books, 1992), 1

2 Daniel C. Maguire, *A Moral Creed for All Christians* (Minneapolis: Fortress Press, 2005), 57.

3 Marcus J. Borg, *The Heart of Christianity* (New York: HarperCollins, 2003), 201.

4 See Sallie King, *Being Benevolence: The Social Ethics of Engaged Buddhism* (Honolulu: University of Hawaii Press, 2005).

5 See chapter nine for more detailed discussion of Dr. Ambedkar.

6 See https://www.census2011.co.in/sexratio.php

7 Swami Nirvedananda, *Hinduism at a Glance* (Calcutta: Ramakrishna Mission, 1979), 172. Emphasis added.

8 See CUBh 5.10.8, 272.

9 D. S. Sarma, *The Essence of Hinduism* (Mumbai: Bharatiya Vidya Bhavan 1971), 54.

10 Swami Viditatmananda, *Hindu Dharma* (Ahmedabad: Adhyatma Vidya Mandir, 2008), 92.

11 See Patrick Olivelle, *Saṃnyāsa Upaniṣads: Hindu Scriptures on Asceticism and Renunciation* (New York: Oxford University Press, 2006).

12 See V. D. Savarkar, *Hindutva* (New Delhi: Bharti Sahitya Sadan, 1989).

13 Savarkar, *Hindutva*, 89-90.

14 Savarkar, *Hindutva*, 100-101.

15 See Rambachan, *The Advaita Worldview*, 76-78.

16 CW 1: 20.

17 CW 2: 146

18 CW 2: 150.

19 CW 3: 140

20 CW 5: 137.

21 M. K. Gandhi, *The Voice of Truth* (Ahmedabad: Navajivan, 1969), 124.

22 Gandhi, *The Voice of Truth*, 114.

23 Gandhi, *All Men Are Brothers*, 63.

24 Gandhi, *All Men Are Brothers*, 68.

CHAPTER NINE

ARE THERE PRINCIPLES IN THE HINDU TRADITION CONSONANT WITH LIBERTY, EQUALITY AND FRATERNITY? : *BHAGAVADGĪTĀ* 4:13 AND THE CASTE SYSTEM

Communities across our world continue to struggle for dignity, freedom and equality. We witness the resistance and cries in these communities against those who deny their dignity and who support unjust and historically entrenched social structures. Religious traditions, in some of their teachings, interpretations and practices, have not consistently championed the equal dignity and value of all human beings. In addition, what obtains on the ground in practice does not always reflect the ideals of the tradition. As Charles Kimball reminds us, "It is all too human to compare the ideal version of one's own religion with the visibly flawed lived reality of other religions–a tendency found in all traditions."[1] In addressing moral issues from the perspective of our traditions, it is imperative that our articulation of religious ideals be accompanied by a rigorous self-criticism that is willing to interrogate teachings and structures that devalue human beings and deny their dignity.

In what follows, I will examine the *cāturvarṇa* or the caste order of Hindu society in relation to the aspiration for dignity and equality for all human beings. Is the caste system compatible with such an ideal? The Hindu tradition is complex and diverse, and for the purpose of a focused discussion, I will concentrate on the *Bhagavadgītā* and on India post-independence. The thirteenth verse of chapter four in the *Bhagavadgītā* is a seminal and significant text for Hindu discussions on caste. The speaker here is Śrī Krishna, widely regarded by Hindus as a manifestation (*avatāra*) on earth of the divine.

> The four *varṇas* were created by Me, differentiated by qualities (*guṇa*) and action (*karma*); although I am the creator, know Me to be the immutable non-doer.[2]

I will also highlight salient arguments against some of these interpretations offered by the Dalit leader, Dr. B. R. Ambedkar (1891–1956).[3] I will conclude with constructive Hindu theological claims for the overcoming of caste.

Caste: Past and Present

Though the origins of caste are disputed among historians and scholars of religion, it is clear, from the evidence of the *Ṛg Veda*, regarded as the earliest of the four Vedas, that there was an early division between those who thought of and referred to themselves as *ārya* (noble, of noble descent, pure), and defined themselves over and against others referred to as *dasyus*. The *dasyus* were considered as subhuman, hypocritical, without virtue, observing different customs and likened to a famine.[4]

Evidence suggests that by around 800 BCE, those regarding themselves as *āryas* had consolidated themselves in relation to other groups and systematized their relationship in the form of a hierarchically structured system (*varṇa*). The *brāhmaṇas* (priests) occupied the top, followed by the *rājanya* or *kṣatriya* (soldiers), *vaiśyas* (merchants and farmers), and *śūdras* (laborers). The first three groups were regarded as the *dvijas* or twice-born and were entitled to perform and participate in Vedic ritual. Generally, only male members of these *varṇas* underwent the initiatory ritual (*upanayana*) that enabled them to study the Vedas. The incorporation of the *śūdras* into the *varṇa* system, and especially their subservient role in relation to the other groups, supports the hypothesis that they represent the "others" who were gradually included into the complex social order. It is also possible that a policy of appeasement was practised, that rewarded cooperative groups with elevation to membership in the upper *varṇas*.[5]

Not all groups, however, were assimilated and incorporated. It is likely that some groups resisted or were not offered the "privilege" of becoming part of the hierarchical order. Such groups, such as the *cāṇḍālas* and *śvapacas*, were declared ritually impure (*aśuchi*) and segregated. The *cāṇḍālas* were equated with animals and considered unfit even to eat the remnants of others' meals. By the time of Manu (ca.150 BCE), it was believed that birth into a particular caste was the consequence of *karma* or the maturation of past moral actions in the present life. From its early use to refer to a specific group, *cāṇḍāla* became a general term for the untouchable other.

Numerous injunctions, based on general features of the *varṇa* system such as the polarity of purity and impurity, hereditary occupations, and the idea of the *dvija* (twice-born) led to the institution of practices against those groups now branded as *asprśya* (lit. untouchable). By the period between 400 BCE–400 CE, standard features of untouchability such as physical segregation, non-commensality and non-connubiality were firmly in place. The Vedas were not to be studied in a village where *cāṇḍālas* resided. Food offered in ritual was defiled if seen by a *cāṇḍāla* and sacrificial vessels were rendered impure by their touch. The texts specifying prohibitions against the *cāṇḍālas* grouped them with animals.[6]

Today, the untouchables are designated in the Indian Constitution as belonging to the Scheduled Castes. Based on the most recent Indian census (2011), members of the Scheduled Castes and Scheduled Tribes constitute twenty-five percent of India's population.[7] The Scheduled Castes alone number over 200 million. The Constitution of independent India abolished untouchability and forbids discrimination on the basis of caste, but it did not abolish caste itself as a social institution. Special laws, such as the Protection of Civil Rights Act, 1976, have been enacted to give meaning to the constitutional provisions.

Changes though occurring at a slow pace, are underway. The impact of legislation, urban life, democracy, freedom, equality, and feminism are transforming age-old attitudes and customs. In addition, the modern era is also witness to increasing political self-awareness among the untouchables and their readiness to organize themselves to agitate for justice. It is also true that laws prohibiting caste discrimination are poorly administered. The phenomenon of untouchability persists in contemporary India and Hindus continue to define the meaning of Hindu identity over and against those who are deemed polluting and, for this reason, marginalized. The sharp distinctions between self and other, the boundaries of the pure and impure, are still drawn sharply in Indian villages, where the character of human and economic relationships is still governed by the hierarchies of caste and where reports of violence against persons of lower castes are common. Although the conditions of life in Indian cities are quite different from those obtaining in rural areas, cities are not free from the travails of caste and untouchability. In urban areas, discrimination expresses itself in more subtle forms and in limited job choices, that push untouchables into menial tasks.

Caste is a complex social system that intersects with all dimensions of the lives of those whose identities are formed and defined by its categories and its hierarchical ordering of human beings. The value that it confers on those in its upper ranks is in relation to the devaluing of those who are regarded as lower. Devaluation leads to the perception of people as objects and not as fellow beings who feel and suffer like us. It provides the conditions for guilt-free violence and mistreatment.

Whatever its hoary origins, it is also true that caste, despite the efforts of several Hindu teachers and reformers, perpetuated itself with religious legitimation and many regard the practice of caste as a religious obligation. Hindu leadership is still dominated by male persons from the upper castes, who have always experienced power and privilege within the tradition. Having never experienced religiously justified oppression and injustice, they assume, wrongly, that the tradition that has been good to them is good for all who are born within its fold. They resist the questioning of a system that guarantees them power and privilege.

What are contemporary Hindu teachers and commentators (*bhāṣyakāra*) of sacred texts saying today about caste and religion? To answer this question, I examine select influential commentators and focus on their exegesis of *Bhagavadgītā* 4:13. These works are in English or available in English translations.

CONTEMPORARY COMMENTATORS:

Jayadayal Goyandka

Jayadayal Goyandka's (1885–1965) commentary on the *Bhagavadgītā* (*Śrīmadbhagavadgītā Tattvavivekcanī*) is one of the best known and widely circulated commentaries. It is published by the Gita Press, Gorakhpur, the largest publisher and distributor of low-priced Hindu religious texts.[8] Goyandaka's commentary is in its seventeenth edition.[9]

Goyandka, like most of the commentators we will discuss, identifies the qualities (*guṇa*) in *Bhagavadgītā* 4:13 with the three fundamental constituents of matter (*prakṛti*) as expounded in the Saṁkhya philosophical tradition. These constituents are *sattva* (associated with pleasure, light, and knowledge), *rajas* (associated with energy and activity) and *tamas* (associated with passivity, ignorance and indifference).[10] The nature of the individual, according to Goyandka, is determined by the proportion of these qualities, and this proportion, in turn, results from the actions performed by each person in the course of previous births. Those in whom the quality of *sattva* predominates are born as *brāhmaṇas;* those in whom the quality of *rajas* predominates are born as *kṣatriyās;* those in whom the quality of *rajas* predominates (followed by *tamas*) are born as *vaiśyas;* and those in whom the quality of *tamas* predominates (followed by *rajas*) are born as *śudras.* God, explains Goyandka, on the basis on these qualities, ordains the birth of persons in the appropriate caste group and specifies the duties that are in consonance with their *guṇa* disposition.[11]

Goyandka is quite clear on what is required for the proper working of this social system.

> So long as purity of blood is maintained, so long as procreation takes place through the union of parents of the same order and there is no admixture of blood due to the union of heterogeneous elements, the system of classification of society as set forth above goes on unimpaired.[12]

In determining the caste status of a person, asks Goyandka, should we give priority to birth or to actions? Ideally, he answers, a person is qualified to membership in a caste when he is born into that caste and follows the prescribed actions. Goyandka, however, privileges and gives priority to birth.

> But the ruling factor is birth; hence birth should be recognized as the basis of classifying the *varṇas*. If the parents of an individual belong to the same caste and no confusion of castes in any form is allowed to take place in the matter of birth, no confusion of duties will easily ensue in ordinary circumstance.[13]

Salvation is contingent on following divinely ordained caste duties.

> For instance, if he who is a *brāhmana* by birth does not follow the rules of conduct prescribed for a *brāhmana*, he cannot attain salvation; on the other hand, if a *śudra*, though of good conduct and practicing self-control as a duty common to all follows the vocation of a *brāhmana*, and earns his living by following the same, he incurs sin.[14]

In his commentary on *Bhagavadgītā* 4:13, Goyandka affirms the determination of caste status on the basis of birth, the necessity for caste-endogamy, and hereditary occupations. The only feature of the caste system that he laments is deviation from caste duties caused by what he identifies as "undesirable association, impure diet and a wrong type of education and culture."

Swami Chinmayananda

Swami Chinmayananda (1916–1993) is the founder of the Chinmaya Mission (1953), one of the most successful worldwide Hindu organizations following the tradition of Advaita Vedānta as systematized by Śaṅkara.[15] The organization administers Sandeepany Sadhanalaya (Mumbai), a modern institute that runs Vedānta study courses.

Like Goyandka, Chinmayananda understands "qualities" to refer to the three *guṇas*. The *guṇas* determine human temperament and, on the basis of distinctions in temperament, human beings have been classified into four *varṇas*.[16] Chinmayananda likens this classification to trade or professional divisions in a city. The ideal is one of complementarity and cooperation, and not competition. Chinmayananda laments the fact that this ideal was lost "in the power politics of the early middle-ages in India," and *brahmin* interpreters emphasized only the first quarter of verse 13, "The four *varṇas* were created by Me." They intentionally ignored the second quarter that identifies the basis of the classification to be what he refers to as "mental quality and physical action."

Unlike Goyandka, Chinmayananda argues against birth as a determinant of caste status. The primary determinants are one's thoughts and actions, based on the preponderance of the *guṇas*.

> The definition insists that he alone is a *Brahmana,* whose thoughts are as much *Sattwic,* as his actions are. A *Kshatriya* is one who is *Rajasic* in his thoughts and actions. A *Sudra* is not only one whose thoughts are *Tamasic,* but he also lives a life of low endeavors, for satisfying his base animal passions and flesh-appetites.[17]

Swami Chinmayananda is not opposed to the basic categories of caste as a social arrangement. His contention is with birth as the determinative factor, and this he regards as the consequence of *brahmin* manipulation of the text.

Swami Dayananda Saraswati

Swami Dayananda Saraswati (1930–2015) is a former disciple of Swami Chinmayananda. In 1986, he founded the Arsha Vidya Gurukulam, also devoted to the study of the Advaita Vedānta in the tradition of Śaṅkara. The organization runs centers in various parts of India and abroad, dedicated to Advaita teaching and the training of teachers. Swami Dayananda's commentary on the *Bhagavdgītā* is one of the most extensive historically. It is currently published in nine volumes and intended to be used as a home study course.[18]

Like Chinmayananda, Dayananda emphasizes that the division described in 4:13 is based on psychological qualities and he understands this division to have universal applicability.[19]

> In the Vedic context, people having the first combination, *sattva-rajas-tamas,* are called *brāhmaṇas,* those having the second combination, *rajas-sattva-tamas*, are called *kṣatriyas*, those having the third, *rajas-tamas-sattva*, are called *vaiśyas*, and those having the fourth combination, *tamas- rajas-sattva*, are called *śūdras.*[20]

Caste names, Dayananda contends, should be determined by the work a person does, "regardless of which group he or she is born into."

> A person who is born into a *brāhmaṇa* family but does *vaiśya-karma,* is a *vaiśya.* A true *brāhmaṇa,* on the other hand, is one who, having been born into a *brāhmaṇa* family, lives a simple life so as not to exploit the society, studies and teaches the Veda, and performs the obligatory rituals for the welfare of the people, just as his grandfather and great grandfather did before him.[21]

Dayananda, however, seems to have a preference for hereditary occupations. In a society where the concept of duty associated with different groups is clear, "The person need not choose a vocation in life. He or she knows exactly what is to be done based on which family he or she is born into. One's duty is written over one's forehead at birth, so to speak."[22] If one believes in the law of *karma,* states Dayananda, one is likely to see one's birth as the consequence of *karma,* and duties become clear. One will not wish for any other work. The concept of duty, however, he argues, does not work well in a system where the main objective is wealth. People are likely to change vocations on the basis of better salaries. If liberation, on the other hand, is the goal of one's life, one is likely to happily perform one's hereditary occupation in an attitude of worship (*karma-yoga*), without thoughts of superiority or inferiority. Royal families protected the fourfold order in India, but it was destroyed during the centuries of Muslim rule.[23]

A. C. Bhaktivedanta Swami Prabhupada

A.C. Bhaktivedanta Swami Prabhupada (1896–1977) is the founder of the International Society for Krishna Consciousness (1966), a modern devotional movement in the tradition of Gauḍīya Vaiṣṇavism, centered on the worship of Krishna. Theologically Gauḍīya Vaiṣṇavism aligns itself with the qualified nondual teaching of Rāmānuja (11 CE), distinguishing itself from the nondualism of Śaṅkara. Bhaktivedanta reads *Bhagavadgītā* 4:13 as affirming the divine origin of "the four divisions of the social order."[24]

> He is therefore the creator of the four divisions of the social order, beginning with the intelligent class of men, technically called the *brāhmaṇas* due to their being situated in the mode of goodness. Next is the administrative class, technically called the *kṣatriyas* due to their being situated in the mode of passion. The mercantile men, called the *vaiśyas* are situated in the mixed modes of passion and ignorance, and the *śūdras*, or the laborer class are situated in the ignorant mode of material nature.[25]

The purpose of the fourfold social order is the elevation of human beings, culminating in devotion to Krishna and becoming a Vaiṣṇava.

The Vaiṣṇava is higher than the *brāhmaṇa*, since the latter only knows an impersonal absolute and not Krishna, as the "Supreme Personality of Godhead." Though coming from a different theological lineage, Prabhupada's reading of *Bhagavadgītā* 4:13 does not differ substantially from the Advaita readings cited above. One's location in the social order, argues Prabhupada, does not matter if one's work is offered worshipfully to Krishna.[26]

Sarvapalli Radhakrishnan

Sarvapalli Radhakrishnan (1888–1975), philosopher and former President of India, also reads the verse as classifying human beings on the basis of aptitude and function, and not birth (*jāti*). The fourfold order, according to Radhakrishnan, is intended for human evolution, even though he does not specify how it accomplishes this purpose. Radhakrishnan laments the present "morbid condition of India broken into castes and subcastes," noting that this state is "opposed to the unity taught by the *Gītā*, which stands for an organic as against an atomistic conception of society."[27] Perplexingly, Radhakrishnan cites the argument of Yudhiṣṭhira in the Māhabhārata that the proliferation of intercaste marriages makes it difficult to identify caste identity on the basis of birth. This leaves conduct as the only determining factor.

Commentarial Consensus

These post-independence commentators on the *Bhagavadgītā* have much in common. The major issue of difference is whether caste is determined by birth (*jāti*) or by quality (*guṇa*) and action (*karma*). Goyandka privileges birth. Other commentators emphasize qualities and action, while lamenting the difficulty of applying the criteria of birth. The following are some of the areas of agreement among the commentators.

First, none of the commentators problematize the text itself. They treat the fourfold order as divinely ordained. There is no attempt to situate the text in historical context or understand caste as a human-created institution.

Second, all of the commentators seem to treat the fourfold order as the reality on the ground. Radhakrishnan has a single reference to "outcaste," but does not comment in any detail on this category. The fact that there are over 200 million persons, by today's figures, marginalized and devalued as untouchables, is not discussed. Commentators describe an idealized fourfold order, ignoring how the system, in reality, functions. The heated debates around the issues of caste and untouchability in the years leading up to independence do not inform these commentaries. Radhakrishnan's commentary was published first in 1948, just one year after independence. No commentator, including M. K. Gandhi, cites the views or writings of Dr. B. R. Ambedkar (1891–1956), the most famous Dalit leader, or any other Dalit writer.[28] The readings are remarkably ahistorical.

Third, there is no acknowledgement in these commentaries of the dehumanization, indignities, and injustices inflicted on the untouchables. There is no owning of responsibility or expression of regret for their suffering.

Fourth, some of our commentators suggest that one's place in the caste order does not or should not matter if one's aim is liberation and one performs one's work worshipfully. The argument, as stated by A. C. Bhaktivedanta Swami Prabhupada, that one's place in the social order does not matter if one performs actions in a spirit of worship is, to say the least, deeply disturbing. It legitimizes a particular order, however unjust it may be, and discourages dissent. It commends a pursuit of liberation (*mokṣa*) that makes engagement with issues of social justice irrelevant.

Fifth, various commentators commend the ideal relationship among castes to be one of complementarity and cooperation, and not competition. This, however, easily conceals the underlying inequalities. Complementarity of roles does not require justice or equality. Swami Chidbhavananda, for example, though arguing for a caste order based on qualities and actions, commends the system for eliminating competition.

> The *varṇa dharma* is the last word on an ideal social order. India has evolved this system to its perfection. It cuts at the root of the cruel competition with its attendant evils. It offers instead, an attitude of self-dedication crowned with renunciation. Every time India was faithful to this philosophical basis of her social order, she emerged as a heaven on earth.[29]

It is not clear how a *guṇa* based order eliminates competition, unless he has in mind a system of hereditary occupation that does not allow for freedom of choice.

Sixth, none of our commentators interrogate the necessity for the categories and terminology of caste. Some liken caste to trade divisions and emphasize its universal applicability. Caste duties should be performed, it is argued, without feelings of superiority and inferiority. The fact is that caste is hierarchical and the language of our commentators reflect this fact. The *guṇa* of *tamas* which supposedly predominates in *śudras*, is associated with passivity, indifference and ignorance. *Śudras*, according to A.C. Bhaktivedanta Swami Prabhupada, are "situated in the ignorant mode of material nature." One commentator speaks of a mental evolution from "*śūdra*hood" to "*brāhmaṇa*hood."[30] Why would anyone want to self-describe as *śudra*? The terminology of *varṇa* is so saturated with assumptions of purity and impurity, and superiority and inferiority, that it is impossible to see how it could be deployed otherwise or how such a classification contributes to human flourishing and the common good.

Seventh, all of our commentators, with the exception of Goyandka, assume that the major problem of the *varṇa* system is the use of birth as the determinant of *varṇa,* rather than qualities and action. The assumption appears to be that if human beings are classified on the basis of qualities and actions, problems will be overcome and the social good served. In the words of Swami Chinmayananda, "Just as, in a metropolis, on the basis of trade or professions, we divide people as doctors, advocates, professors, traders, politicians, tongawalas, etc., so too on the basis of the different texture of thoughts entertained by the intelligent creatures, the four 'castes' had been labelled in the past."[31] This argument is usually accompanied by emphasizing that these four groups should be in cooperative relationships. This is a pro-*varṇa* argument that is also associated particularly with the reformist Arya Samaj movement, founded in 1875 by Swami Dayananda Saraswati (1824–1883).

Ambedkar's Challenge of *Cāturvarṇa*

These interpretations of the meaning of *cāturvarṇa* are carefully contested by Dr. B. R. Ambedkar. It is highly regrettable that these interpretations continue to be proffered without any attention to the sharp criticisms of Dr. Ambedkar. I have already noted the absence of engagement with Dr. Ambedkar by post-independence *Bhagavadgītā* commentators.[32] One of the sad consequences of this is that commentators continue to repeat interpretations that were thoughtfully challenged by Dr. Ambedkar. It is significant, of course, that all of these commentators come from upper caste backgrounds. Here, I will highlight six of Dr. Ambedkar's arguments against the *guṇa-karma* validation of caste.

First, Ambedkar interrogates the necessity for *varṇa* labels. "The names Brahmin, Kshatriya, Vaishya and Shudra," writes Dr. Ambedkar, "are names which are associated with a definite and fixed notion in the mind of every Hindu. This notion is that of a hierarchy based on birth."[33] As long as these names are retained, the hierarchies of higher and lower, deeply embedded in them, will persist. The commentators we discussed seem to think that the terminology of caste could be employed without the hierarchy of caste.

Second, Ambedkar raises a very pragmatic challenge: "How are you going to compel people who have acquired the higher status based on birth, without reference to their worth, to vacate that status?" Will they ever recognize as equal those who are currently classified lower on the basis on birth but who deserve a higher status on the basis of worth?[34] In other words, who classifies and enforces?

Third, Ambedkar objects to the very ideal of a fourfold classification of human beings. The diversity, richness and flexibility of human nature make it impossible to classify us all into four groups. "Chaturvarnya must fail for the very reason for which Plato's Republic must fail—namely, that it is not possible to pigeon men into holes according to class."[35]

Fourth, *cāturvarṇa* makes groups unreasonably dependent on each other for the fulfillment of vital needs. Groups suffer when other groups do not pursue their vocations or fail to fulfill their responsibilities to other groups. The *śudra* is particularly vulnerable in this system, since he is prohibited from wealth, knowledge and arms. "Education, everyone must have. Means of defense, everyone must have. These are the paramount requirements of every man for his self-preservation. How can the fact that his neighbor is educated and armed help a man who is uneducated and disarmed?"[36]

Fifth, Ambedkar raises important questions related to status of women within this system. Are women classified on the basis of worth or do they assume the *varṇa* of their husbands? Assuming the *varṇa* status of their husbands defeats the ideal of a classification based on worth.

Sixth, how will such a system be enforced? "The system of chaturvarnya must perpetually face the problem of the transgressor. Unless there is a penalty attached to the act of transgression, men will not keep to their respective classes. The whole system will break down, being contrary to human nature. Chaturvarnya cannot subsist by its own inherent goodness. It must be enforced by law."[37]

Liberty, Equality and Fraternity

In enunciating the principles that are necessary for the flourishing of any human community, Ambedkar highlighted liberty, equality and fraternity. All of these, however, he argued, were absent in the Hindu tradition. In his exposition of these values, Ambedkar turned to the French philosopher and political thinker, Jacques Maritain (1882–1973). He quotes Maritain in his essay, "The Hindu Social Order: Its Essential Principles."

> To say that a man is a person is to say that in the depth of his being he is more a whole than a part and more independent than servile. It is to say that he is a minute fragment of matter that is at the same time a universe, a beggar who participates in the absolute being, mortal flesh whose value is external and a bit of straw into which heaven enters. It is this metaphysical mystery that religious thought designates when it says that the person is the image of God. The value of the person, his dignity and rights belong to the order of things naturally sacred which bear the imprint of the Father of Being, and which have in him the end of their movement.[38]

Of the three principles necessary for human flourishing, Ambedkar gave pride of place to fraternity, as sustaining both liberty and equality. He equated it with what the Buddha spoke of as *maitrī* and, in fact, expressed a preference for the Sanskrit term. He believed that fraternity had its roots in a religious worldview, as his citation from Maritain shows. He was convinced that caste injustice and oppression were intrinsic to Hinduism. The Hindu social order, wrote Ambedkar, "refuses to recognize that men no matter how profoundly they differ as individuals in capacity and character, are equally entitled as human beings to considerations and respect and that the well-being of a society is likely to be increased if it so plans its organization that, whether their powers are great or small, all its members may be equally enabled to make the best of such powers as they possess. It will not allow equality of circumstances, institutions and manner of life. It is against equalitarian temper."[39]

The Hindu tradition, according to Ambedkar needed a teaching that justified and supported the values of liberty, equality and fraternity. Are there such teachings within the tradition? Ambedkar himself, without elaboration, hinted at such teachings in his *Annihilation of Caste*.

> I am no authority on the subject. But I am told that for such principles as will be consonant with liberty, equality and fraternity, it may not be necessary for you to borrow from foreign sources, and that you could draw for such principles on the Upanishads. Whether you could do so without a complete remoulding, a considerable scraping and chipping off from the ore they contain, is more than I can say. This means a complete change in the fundamental notions of life. It means a complete change in the values of life. It means a complete change in outlook and in attitude towards men and things.[40]

This is not a task that Ambedkar himself was willing to undertake. On October 14, 1956, in the city of Nagpur, Dr. Ambedkar converted to Buddhism. The following day, he delivered an address in the city explaining his reasons. Seven weeks after his conversion, Dr. Ambedkar passed away at the age of 64. He was clearly disillusioned and pessimistic about the possibilities for reform and rejuvenation within the Hindu tradition. At heart was his conviction that the tradition does not teach equality and that the Buddha was one of the rare teachers of India to advocate equality. The Buddha, Ambedkar believed, focused centrally on suffering and its overcoming.

> We will go by our path; others should go by their path. We have found a new way. This is a day of hope. This is a way of success, of prosperity. This way is not something new. This path was not brought here from somewhere else. This path is from here; it is purely Indian. The Buddhist religion has been in India for two thousand years. Truly speaking, we regret that we did not become Buddhists before this. The principles spoken by Bhagvan Buddha are immortal.[41]

Where does Ambedkar see the light of hope in the Hindu tradition on matter of fraternity? In an essay titled, "Brahma is Not Dharma: What Good is Brahma?" Ambedkar grants that the Hindu tradition offers a teaching with redemptive possibilities.[42] He names it as "Brahmaism," and says that it "had greater potentialities for producing social democracy *than* the idea of fraternity."[43] He locates the source of this teaching in the *Upaniṣad* texts: "That Thou Art (*tat tvam asi*)" (*Chāndogya Upaniṣad* 6.8.7); "I am *brahma* (*ahaṁ brahmāsmi*)" (*Bṛhadāraṇyaka Upaniṣad* 1.4.10); and "All this is Brahma (*sarvam khalvidam brahma)*" (*Chāndogya Upaniṣad* 3.14.1). Brahmaism, according to Ambedkar, affirms (i) the identity between *ātmā* and Brahma*;* (ii) that the reality behind the world is Brahma; and (iii) everything is of the essence of Brahma.[44] Ambedkar welcomed what he read as the affirmation of human worth in the "I am Brahma" declaration. It is not an arrogant assertion.

> Those who sneer at *Aham Brahmasmi* (I am Brahma*)* as an impudent utterance forget the other part of the Mahavakya, namely *Tattvamasi* (thou art also Brahma). If *Aham Brahmasmi* had stood alone without the conjunct of *Tattvamasi,* it may have been possible to sneer at it. But with the conjunct of *Tattvamasi*, the charge of selfish arrogance cannot stand against Brahmaism.[45]

This teaching, contended Ambedkar, affirming the equal worth and value of every human being provides a strong foundation for democracy. "If all persons are parts of Brahma then all are equal and all must enjoy the same liberty, which is what democracy means."[46] The problem of Brahmaism is not its teaching but its failure to connect theology with life; to "return to society as instruments of re-constructing society." He chastises Śaṅkara for perpetuating this great chasm between teaching and social reality.

> What is more ridiculous is the teaching of the Great Shankaracharya. For it was this Shankaracharya who taught that there is Brahma and this Brahma is real and pervades all and at the same time upheld all the inequities of the Brahmanic society.[47]

Ambedkar's experience of the Hindu tradition as based on graded inequality is undeniable. His intuition about the *Upaniṣads* as the sources of principles for re-envisioning and reforming Hindu society is correct, even though he was not optimistic and did not think it was his responsibility to undertake this work. I share Dr. Ambedkar's belief that the *Upaniṣads* provide a theological basis for the equal worth and dignity of all human beings and for the refutation of the assumptions of inequality, impurity, and indignity that are the foundations of caste. These principles also provide the insights and values for advocating for justice.

The *Upaniṣads* speak of *brahman,* the ultimate reality, as "That from which all beings originate, by which they are sustained and to which they return (*Taittirīya Upaniṣad* 3.1.1). Other *Upaniṣads* speak of *brahman* as the indivisible and uncreated One from which the many are created (*Chāndogya Upaniṣad* 6.2.1-2). The *Upaniṣads* affirm unreservedly the equal existence of *brahman* in all. *Īśa Upaniṣad* begins with the famous call to see everything in the world of movement as pervaded by *Īśa* (God). There is no life outside of God and there is nothing that exists which is not sustained by God. The equal presence of God in all beings is the source of the inherent dignity and equal worth of every human being. It is our antidote to any effort to deny the personhood, worth and dignity of another. The implication is that we cannot honor and value the ultimate and devalue human beings. We cannot give our assent or support to any social or cultural system that is founded on human inequality and indignity. Our understanding of ultimate reality requires diligence and discernment in identifying such systems and in articulating critiques from our theological centers. Caste inequality is a blatant denial of the equal existence of the divine in everyone. We must, as Ambedkar challenges us, connect theology with life.

The positive implications of this teaching are just as important as the rejection of inequality and injustice in caste. The single value and practice that expresses best the meaning of this teaching is compassion (*dayā*). In the *Bṛhadāraṇyaka Upaniṣad* 5.2.1, compassion is commended, along with control (*dama*) and generosity (*datta*), by the teacher to his students on the day of their graduation. Control is the unique human ability to consider the common good in all actions and to desist from causing suffering to others. Giving is the joyous and abundant sharing of one's gifts as an expression of gratitude. Compassion is the identification with others in joy and in sorrow. The teacher does not specify a recipient of our control, generosity and compassion. The point is that these virtues must be expressed in our relationship with every being.

Connecting theology with life, as Ambedkar recommends, requires that we expand our understanding of human suffering. The traditional emphasis has been on suffering as an inward condition associated with ignorance (*avidyā*). We see the implications of this narrow understanding in the argument that caste status does not matter as long as one performs actions in a spirit of worship. Love of God, in other words, is entirely compatible with living indifferently in a social order characterized by inequality. There is no good reason, however, to limit the meaning of suffering in this way. We must not ignore the suffering of human beings when they lack opportunities to attain the necessities for dignified and decent living or when suffering is inflicted through oppression and injustice based on caste, gender or race. It is not acceptable to affirm teachings about life's unity in *brahman* while being indifferent to inequality and oppression at the social level. Love of God must inspire engagement with the world and not apathy. Working to overcome suffering requires identifying those political, social and economic and religious structures that cause and perpetuate suffering. Suffering in all forms matter.

We will not undertake this work until we are willing, in the Hindu tradition, to acknowledge the reality of injustice, past and present. We need to be more self-critical and less defensive and to hold our traditions accountable to their highest teachings. Citing the injustices of other traditions does not justify or excuse those within our own. We must be attentive to the voices of those who experience our tradition as oppressive and unjust and as denying them dignity, power and freedom. We must be willing to hear these truths, however challenging and difficult. In the absence of such acknowledgement and attentiveness, we will continue to perpetuate teachings about caste that perpetuate suffering. Causing suffering to others *(hiṃsā)* and indifference to such suffering are the antithesis of what the Hindu tradition advocates at its highest ethical ideal of nonviolence *(ahiṃsā)*.

References

1 Charles Kimball, *When Religion Becomes Evil* (San Francisco: HarperCollins Publishers, 2002), 27.

2 *chātur-varṇyaṁ mayā sṛiṣṭaṁ guṇa-karma-vibhāgaśhaḥ tasya kartāram api māṁ viddhyakartāram avyayam*. My translation.

3 Bhimrao Ramji Ambedkar was born in 1891 into the Mahar caste, one of the largest untouchable castes in the state of Maharashtra. As a child, he experienced the humiliation of untouchability in its many forms. Barbers refused to cut his hair, cart-drivers would not transport him, and teachers denied him the opportunity to study Sanskrit, forced him to sit on the ground and refused to touch his books. With amazing perseverance, Ambedkar became the first untouchable to enter university, graduating from Elphinstone College in 1908 with a degree in economics and political science. With a scholarship from the State of Baroda, Ambedkar attended Columbia University in New York, completing a Master's Degree and then a PhD in economics. He also studied at the London School of Economics earning a DSc degree in economics. He was admitted to the British bar as a barrister. Upon his return to India, Ambedkar devoted himself to combating the injustices of untouchability, eventually rising to become independent India's first Law Minister and chairman of the drafting committee for the Constitution of India. Ambedkar resigned from Nehru's Cabinet because of a controversy surrounding the Hindu Code Bill. He was appointed to India's Upper House, the Rajya Sabha, until his death on December 6, 1956, at the age of 65.

4 See Mukherjee, *Beyond the Four Varnas*, 18-19.

5 Mukherjee, *Beyond the Four Varnas,* Chapter 2.

6 For contemporary accounts of growing up as an untouchable in India, see Omprakash Valmiki, *Joothan,* and Narendra Jadhav, *Untouchables.*

7 "SCs, STs form 25% of population, says Census 2011 data."

8 "Gita Press," https://www.britannica.com/topic/Gita-Press#ref1041030.

9 Jayadayal Goyandaka, *Śrīmadbhagavadgītā Tattvavivekcanī* (Gorakhpur: Gita Press, 2002).

10 See Satischandra Chatterjee and Dhirendramohan Datta, *An Introduction to Indian Philosophy*, Chapter 7.

11 These duties are described in *Bhagavadgītā* 18: 41-44.

12 Goyandaka, *Śrīmadbhagavadgītā Tattvavivekcanī*, 198.

13 Goyandaka, *Śrīmadbhagavadgītā Tattvavivekcanī,* 198.

14 Goyandaka, *Śrīmadbhagavadgītā Tattvavivekcanī,* 198

15 See Nancy Patchen, *Journey of a Master: Swami Chinmayananda, the Man, the Path, the Teaching* (Fremont: Asian Humanities Press, 1990).

16 Swami Chinmayananda, *The Holy Geeta* (Bombay: Central Chinmaya Mission Trust,1995), 243.

17 Chinmayananda, *The Holy Geeta,* 244.

18 Swami Dayananda Saraswati, *Bhavagad Gītā*, 9 vols. (Chennai: Arsha Vidya Research, 2011). Though having the same monastic name, he must be distinguished from the founder of the Arya Samaj.

19 Saraswati, *Bhavagad Gītā,* vol. 4, 80.

20 Saraswati, *Bhavagad Gītā,* vol. 4, 84.

21 Saraswati, *Bhavagad Gītā,* vol. 4, 86.

22 Saraswati, *Bhavagad Gītā,* vol. 4, 87

23 Saraswati, *Bhavagad Gītā,* vol. 4, 91

24 See A.C. Bhaktivedanta Swami Prabhupada, *Bhagavadgītā As It Is* (Los Angeles: The Bhaktivedanta Book Trust, 1981), 88.

25 Prabhupada, *Bhagavadgītā As It Is*, 88. The "mode of material nature" refers here also to the three *guṇas.*

26 Prabhupada, *Bhagavadgītā As It Is,* 212-213.

27 S. Radhakrishnan, *Bhagavadgītā* (London: Allen and Unwin, 1963), 161.

28 M. K. Gandhi, *The Bhagavadgita* (Delhi: Orient Paperbacks, n.d).

29 Swami Chidbhavananda, *The Bhagavadgita*, (Tamil Nadu: Sri Ramakrishna Tapovanam, 1982),916.

30 Chidbhavananda, *The Bhagavadgita*, 284.

31 Chinmayananda, *The Holy Geeta*, 234. A tongawala is a driver of the horse-drawn cart.

32 All quotations and references are from B. R. Ambedkar, *Annihilation of Caste.*

33 Ambedkar, *Annihilation of Caste,* 264.

34 Ambedkar, *Annihilation of Caste*, 265.

35 Ambedkar, *Annihilation of Caste*, 267.

36 Ambedkar, *Annihilation of Caste*, 273.

37 Ambedkar, *Annihilation of Caste*, 268.

38 B. R. Ambedkar, *Writings and Speeches*, vol. 3, comp. Vasant Moon (Bombay: Education Department, Government of Maharashtra, 1987), 96.

39 Ambedkar, *Writings and Speeches*, 106.

40 Ambedkar, *Annihilation of Caste*, 311.

41 http://www.columbia.edu/itc/mealac/pritchett/00ambedkar/txt_ambedkar_conversion.html.

42 See B. R. Ambedkar, *Riddles in Hinduism: The Annotated Critical Selection*, ed. Kancha Ilaiah (New Delhi: Navayana Publishing, 2016),

43 Ambedkar, *Riddles in Hinduism*, 172.

44 Ambedkar, *Riddles in Hinduism*, 175.

45 Ambedkar, *Riddles in Hinduism*, 176.

46 Ambedkar, *Riddles in Hinduism*, 177.

47 Ambedkar, *Riddles in Hinduism*, 179.

CHAPTER TEN

PEACEMAKING AND RECONCILIATION IN HINDUISM

Introduction

In his famous version of the life story of Rama, Śrī Rāmacaritamānas, the Hindi poet, Tulasidasa (ca.16 CE), employs a striking example to highlight the contrast in conduct between saintly and unsaintly persons. He likens the saint to a sandalwood tree and the unsaintly to an axe. Even when the axe cuts or fells the sandal tree, it is saturated with the fragrance of the latter. It is the nature of the sandalwood tree to exude and share its soothing fragrance and this defining quality is not altered by the behavior of the other. The cruelty and injustice of the axe cannot provoke a change in the nature of the sandalwood tree. Like the sandalwood tree, a virtuous person does not become unjust because others are unjust and does not respond with hate towards those who are hate-filled. Goodness is not transformed by an encounter with its opposite.

The urge for reconciliation, motivated by religious considerations, shares a fundamental similarity with the sandalwood tree. It is not transformed by its encounter with hostility and cynicism. It never ceases to share the fragrance of its hope for an inclusive human community where relationships are just and compassionate. Even under the most oppressive conditions, it remains faithful to its vision of a united humanity and gives of itself unselfishly for this end. Why should peacemaking and conflict resolution be concerns of the Hindu tradition? What resources does the tradition offer for overcoming conflict?

These questions become especially significant in the light of the fact that religion is a factor and a contributory cause in many situations of conflict and discord, past and present, active and dormant, in South Asia. Religion, admittedly, is not the sole explanation for any of these conflicts and the religious factor is enmeshed with historical, political, economic, ethnic, and cultural dimensions. Yet, we cannot overlook the role of religion in intensifying narrow loyalties, providing a motivation for violence, and entrenching divisiveness. We cannot also explain away the relationship between religion and violent conflict by the argument that, in all instances, religion is being used or misused for the achievement of power in its various forms. It is too simplistic as well to attribute responsibility for conflict and violence only to what we may regard as extremist elements within religious traditions. The relationship between religion and violence is too ancient to be so easily explained. The divisions between communities are determined not only by geo-political factors, but also by theological considerations, and the latter are often more resistant to change and transformation than the former. When we reflect on the role of religion as a resource for reconciliation, we cannot ignore its continuing contribution to human discord. Discourse about the role of religion in peacemaking has to be self-critical. At the same time, religions are capable of self-correction, adaptation and change. One of the unprecedented opportunities of our present context is the possibility of growth and mutual transformation through interreligious dialogue and encounters.

In spite of the fact that the historical legacy of every religion is a tarnished one, these religions continue to be a potent source of the visions, values and moral energies, which are capable of renewing, transforming and healing human communities. While we must never underestimate and ignore the destructive possibilities of religion, our challenge is also to discover and recover the theological and ethical insights, often ignored and forgotten, which contribute to the well-being of the world community. We may find encouragement and hope in the fact that those religions have survived, which are capable of self-correction, adaptation and change. What are the Hindu theological resources for peacemaking and reconciliation?

Peacemaking and a Shared Identity

We may begin by noting that the will for reconciliation, as well as the possibility of its attainment, are significantly enhanced when parties in conflict are able to affirm some form of shared identity with each other, individual or community. The significance of this truth may be appreciated, from another direction, by noting the extent to which individuals and parties in a conflict often go in emphasizing otherness and denying any common identity. "It is difficult," as Mark Juergensmeyer reminds us, "to belittle and kill a person whom one knows and for whom one has no personal antipathy."[1] The denial of the personhood of the other is a predictable and persistent feature of communities in conflict, past and present. The Irish Protestant leader, Rev. Ian Paisley, spoke of the Pope as "a black-coated bachelor" in his effort to caricature him and the religious community which he leads. The conservative Christian Identity movement in the United States used the term *mudpeople* to describe blacks and Hispanics, and links the Jews with the origins of evil. Jewish and Arab activists in Israel engage in mutual dehumanization and demonization.[2]

One of the central insights of Hinduism, consistently proclaimed by its diverse traditions, is the unity of all existence in God. While this truth is affirmed philosophically in various dialogues of the *Upaniṣads* and in numerous other texts, it is also beautifully expressed in suggestive poetic metaphors and similes. One of the most striking occurs in the *Bhagavadgītā* (7:7) where Krishna likens the divine to the string in a necklace of jewels. "Everything that exists," says Krishna, "is strung on me like jewels on a string." While the gems constituting a necklace may differ individually, the string which runs through each is one and the same. The string links and unites each gem with the other, however separate they are spatially. In an analogous way, God is the common and unifying reality in all created beings, however different each one may be. The Hindu tradition understands God to be the one truth in each one of us, uniting us with each other and with all things.

The nondual tradition of Hinduism (Advaita) articulates the most radical doctrine of the unity of existence in its denial of any ontological dualism and in its view that reality is not-two. *Brahman*, the infinite, constitutes the essential nature of all that exists and is present in all beings as the self (*ātmā*). "The self is *brahman* (*ayam ātmā brahma*)," proclaims the *Māṇḍukya Upanisad* (2). The wise person, according to the *Bhagavadgītā* (6:29), sees the self in all and all in the self.

The significance that Hinduism grants to the truth of life's unity may be appreciated from the fact that its discernment is considered to be the hallmark of wisdom and liberation. We are invited to recognize the sameness of the divine in ourselves and in all beings. The *Bhagavadgīta* (18:20) commends the knowledge which enables a person to see, "one imperishable Being in all beings, undivided in separate beings." Seeing the imperishable and indivisible in the perishable and divided is consequential. It is commended as the highest way of seeing because it is the seeing of that which is ultimate and which, therefore, has ultimate value. The imperishable evokes reverence and that reverence extends to all in which It exists. The outcome of seeing the same God existing identically in all is spoken of as *samadarśinaḥ* (5:18). *Samadarśinaḥ* is seeing with eyes of equality and affirming the equal worth and dignity of every person. A false and inferior way of seeing reality is to regard existing things as isolated, separate and independent of each other and to see in all beings "separate entities of various kinds (18:21)." This Hindu understanding of life's unity is the justification of its regard, in the *Maha Upanishad* (6: 71-72), for the entire world as a single family (*vasudhaiva kutumbakam).* It is also the source of its core values such as *ahiṁsā* (non-injury), *dayā* (compassion) and *dāna* (generosity). Compassion is an integral expression of the vision of life's unity and fundamental interrelatedness.

Understanding life's unity enables us to recognize and celebrate a unity with all beings. This unity is not on the basis of a shared religious identity, ethnicity, culture or nationality. All of these forms of identity also exclude. In this case, however, no one can be excluded, since the divine, which constitutes the unifying truth, does not exclude anyone and anything. "God," as the *Bhagavadgītā* (13:28) puts it, "abides equally in all beings." This is the theological antidote to our human tendency to deny the personhood, worth and dignity of the other.

It is from the perspective of life's unity and our shared unity that we question exploitative and unjust human relationships and structures that foster conflict and divisiveness. It is the same perspective which urges us to overcome estrangement, work for reconciliation and for human relationships that express this central truth of our existence. These relationships must also embody the moral and ethical implications of these truths. *Iśa Upaniṣad* (6) reminds us that the wise person who beholds all beings in the self and the self in all beings does not hate. From the profundity of the Hindu understanding of the nature of life's unity, estrangement from another is estrangement from one's own deepest self and the hate of the other is the hate of one's true self. To be in conflict with another is also to be in conflict with one's self. To inflict suffering on another is to violate one's own self.

Ignorance (*Avidyā*) and Reconciliation

The Hindu tradition assumes that a person who is truly grasped by the truth of life's unity in God will find delight in working for the well-being of others. Ignorance of life's unity, on the other hand, expresses itself in a constricted understanding of self, and in greed, ego-centeredness, violence and exploitation. Although the Hindu tradition must not be simplistic in understanding the causes of human conflict in different parts of our world at different times, it calls attention to the ways in which our understanding of self and other contributes to conflict and violence.

The traditions of Hinduism have almost uniformly described the fundamental human problem to be one of ignorance (*avidyā).* Human conflict and the suffering which it causes are rooted also in a fundamental misunderstanding of the nature of reality. Ignorance, however, can be overcome, and when it is and when we are awakened to the truth of life's unity, there will be a corresponding transformation in the quality of our relationships. There is an optimism about human nature that is not considered to be inherently flawed and defective.

The view that the human problem at its most fundamental level is one of ignorance, and that this ignorance expresses itself in our failure to discern the unity of all existence, is central to the development of a Hindu approach to reconciliation. It enables us to see the other, the one with whom we disagree and with whom we may be locked in struggle, as a fellow human being. It is more difficult to dehumanize or humiliate a person in whom we see ourselves. This approach was at the heart of the Gandhian philosophy and practice of nonviolent resistance (*satyāgraha*). *Satyāgraha* has its limits, but we can learn from that fact that, even in the midst of the strongest disagreements, Gandhi never sought to win support for his case by demonizing his opponent. He understood clearly that when a conflict is constructed sharply in terms of "we" and "they," "victory" and "defeat," the doors to reconciliation and a transformed community are shut. One is left with an enemy, a defeated enemy perhaps, and the next round of the conflict is only postponed. Gandhi included the opponent in the circle of his identity. His grandson describes *satyagraha* as a method that brings together both love and struggle. Gandhi acknowledged that it was easier to free ourselves from fear than from hate.[3]

The Example of Ramana Maharshi

In restraining a disciple from violence towards some thieves who had stolen a few items from his monastery, the saintly Hindu teacher, Ramana Maharishi (1879–1950) asked a provocative question: "They are misguided men and are blinded by ignorance, but let us note what is right and stick to it. If your teeth suddenly bite your tongue, do you knock them out in consequence?"[4] Ramana's question implies the truth of life's unity as well as the reality of ignorance. The teeth and tongue are part of the same body and the biting, however painful, is more in the nature of an error. The consequence is a disposition to compassion and forgiveness, without which reconciliation is impossible. Belief in the goodness of human nature and in ignorance as the source of evil disposes one to an attitude of forgiveness since it orients one to look beyond the immediate action to its underlying causes. We are more likely to respond with hate when we believe that those who hurt us have done so because of intentional malevolence. If we see the action as rooted in ignorance and a flawed understanding of God, self and world, our attitude to the other will be compassionate. We are liberated from hate, bitterness and the desire to inflict pain on the other, and we are open to reconciliation. There is the possibility of peacemaking that is not just the absence of conflict, but a positive embrace of the other.

Ramana's profound sense of his unity with all beings found expression in his spontaneous compassion. He identified in a special way with the poor and the outcasts. He offered water in the oppressive heat of the summer to women from the lower castes, who roamed the mountain gathering grass. He knew that they were hungry and unable to drink from tanks considered to be sacred, for fear of polluting these water sources. Noticing on one occasion that the poor were not fed at the *ashram*, Ramana walked out and stood with them. "If you will not give them food first," said Ramana, "I will not come into the dining hall at all. I will stand under the tree and stretch out my hands for food like them and when I am given a bowl of food, I will eat it, go to straight to the hall and sit."[5] His love expanded to include and embrace animals. He treated the animals in the vicinity of the *ashram* with respect as individuals, seeing each one as an expression of the one reality. He became a friend to them, advocating and protecting them from human aggression and mediating their conflicts. His wisdom about the unity of life made him a natural peacemaker.

The Example of Sita in the Rāmayaṇa

Another fine example of the practice of such compassion and forgiveness occurs in the Rāmayaṇa of Valmiki. After the defeat of Ravana, Hanuman sought the permission of Sita to destroy the female servants of Ravana who had guarded and taunted her during her imprisonment. Sita, however, saw them as victims like herself and offered the superior ideal of forgiveness and reconciliation. "Who would be angry," asks Sita, "with women who are dependent on a monarch who is their superior and who act on other's advice as mere servants or slaves?... I wish in compassion to protect the slaves of Ravana.... A superior being does not render evil for evil.... This is a maxim one should observe; the ornament of virtuous persons is their conduct."[6]

For Tulasidasa, author of the Śrī Rāmacaritamānas, forgiveness and compassion are attributes of the divine in Hinduism. The one quality of Rama, as God, most emphasized by Tulasidasa, is compassion (*kṛpa*). He uses the term "abode of mercy (*kṛpanidhāna*)" on at least five hundred occasions to describe Rama, and has Rama, in the Sundarakāṇḍa (fifth book), making one of the most remarkable statements in the entire text.

> I would not abandon even the murderer of ten million brahmins if he sought refuge in me.

If one keeps in mind that murdering brahmins was regarded as one of the gravest of crimes, the significance of Rama's statement becomes obvious.

Caste and Patriarchy

It is clear that the traditions of Hinduism, in both their distinctive as well as shared insights, provide resources that justify and inspire the work of reconciliation. The challenge for us today is to highlight these core teachings of Hinduism and, more importantly, to simultaneously employ these teachings as the basis of a rigorous Hindu self-examination, which identifies exploitative and oppressive structures. These are the structures which alienate and estrange human beings from each other and from the natural world, and which are fundamentally unjust. It is easy to succumb to the temptation of speaking in enticing and platitudinous ways about the need and value for reconciliation while ignoring the challenges of addressing and overcoming these structures that sanction and enable some human beings to inflict suffering on other human beings. Discourse about reconciliation must not become like a silken robe which conceals a diseased body. Reconciliation will always remain an intangible ideal as long as we are unwilling, from insincerity or fear, to unearth and confront the underlying causes of human conflict and divisiveness. The voices of those within and outside our tradition, who feel despised, rejected and stripped of dignity, must be heard, even in their silence and absence.

The Hindu tradition, like other world religions that developed in patriarchal cultures, reflects assumptions about male gender supremacy, which have been oppressive to Hindu women. Gender justice and reconciliation, therefore, are important tasks to be undertaken by Hindus. The work of gender reconciliation, however, cannot be meaningfully pursued by simply pointing to Hindu teachings about the spiritual equality of men and women or to the presence of feminine images of God. We must ask why a disproportionate percentage of the illiterate in India are women.[7] We must grapple with the reality that women are oppressed when they are forced, because of social values, to abort fetuses merely because the fetus is female. We must question the relationship between the female abortion and the custom of dowry which depletes the economic resources of families into which girls are born, and which makes them feel guilty for being women. The practice of dowry demeans women by signifying that the value of a woman is so low that she becomes acceptable to another only when her family is able to satisfy his greed for the latest gadgets of materialistic fancy. Reconciliation between men and women requires the overcoming of the gender oppressive structures of Hindu society.[8]

Similarly, the inequities of the caste system cannot be addressed only by the offering of concessions to those who have been disadvantaged and who have not traditionally enjoyed the privileges accorded to male members of the upper castes. While supporting such measures, Hindus must also get to the heart of the matter by questioning the very legitimacy of a hierarchical social system which assigns different privileges and value to human beings on the basis of exclusive notions of purity and impurity. The role of religious doctrine and ritual in providing legitimacy for the system of caste must be examined. Reconciliation, from a religious standpoint, cannot be content with the mere amelioration of a questionable system in the interest of social harmony. A self-critical sincerity is needed to acknowledge the ways in which many, especially those from the so-called untouchable castes, experience the tradition as oppressive and as negating their dignity and self-worth. The fact that the religion into which one is born may not be liberative must be admitted.

While an acknowledgment of the past and present indignities of the caste system by those who enjoy its benefits is a necessary step in the process of reconciliation, there must be the will for the reform and reconstruction of Hindu society on the basis of those central insights and values of Hinduism which promote the freedom, dignity and equal worth of human beings. The major traditions of Hinduism are unanimous in their view that the divine exists equally and identically in all beings. While the social implications of this truth are not always consistently and clearly drawn out in the classical texts, all of them articulate it in one way or the other. When the implications for human relationships are enunciated, they are done in terms of a vision of equality and this equality must be the norm by which we critique social structures and gender relationships. The doctrine of divine equality and the worth of all human beings must inspire and impel us to identify and heal the exploitative and oppressive structures of Hindu society. Such work is vital and inseparable to the quest for reconciliation.

Dalit Christians and Hindus: A Case Study

I wish to conclude this chapter with a discussion on the controversy over conversion between Dalit Christians and Hindus, and to offer some suggestions for reconciliation. Members of these communities often have very different memories and understanding about conversion.[9]

Thomas Thangaraj, a Christian theologian, details the story of a group in the southern part of Tamil Nadu from a village named Chanpattu, who converted to Christianity in 1804 and renamed their village, Nazareth. The members were Nadars, a lower caste community. As a low caste group, the Nadars were not allowed to read Hindu scriptures. Conversion to Christianity was a dramatic turnaround for this group. As noted, they changed the name of their village. They also adopted biblical and western names. Debarred from reading the Vedas, Nazareth Christians received the Bible with great joy. For the first time, they joined a voluntary association that they owned and they were in control of its affairs. They were empowered by the fact that they built, owned and used their own place of worship.

The descendants of the Nazareth Christians continue to have a negative view of the Hindu tradition, and seek to emphasize differences with their Hindu neighbors and affirm their distinctive Christian identity. For the Nazareth Christians, conversion to Christianity was an unprecedented opportunity for liberation and religious self-determination. Sathianathan Clarke describes its comprehensive meaning for Dalit Christians.

> Religious conversion for Dalits thus includes a form of boundary smashing and boundary shaping that involves drastic erasure and thorough replacement of inherited but detrimental word-visions and world-ways. It represents a decision away from intra-house options of minimalist tinkering with elements or maximalist transformations with structures of the Hindu vision and way. Rather conversion represents a vociferous NO to the entire religious, social, political and cultural system.[10]

Dalit Christians see conversion as offering freedom from the oppression of caste and for crossing over into a new religious community that affirms social dignity and worth.

Hindu activists and commentators, like Ashok Chowgule, have a diametrically opposed perspective. Chowgule sees conversion as the consequence of an obsession in the Christian tradition and its aggressive methods. After failing to convert Brahmins, according to Chowgule, the Church turned its attention to members of the lower castes.

> Only when they could not make a dent with the Brahmins, did the missionaries turn to the lower castes. The conversions were obtained through inducements and not through any spiritual conviction. They were somewhat successful only when temporal power was with the invading Christians and the area was effectively a colony. The missionaries could project themselves to be benefactors of the lower castes, and ensure that governmental largesse would flow to them.[11]

These perspectives could not be more different. Chowgule denies the agency of the lower castes and sees conversion entirely as the outcome of the power of the missionary and his material inducements. Dalit Christians see their conversion to Christianity as an escape from the violence of caste, psychologically and physically. In the words of Clarke, they embraced "another religious and social framework that valued their own body in relationship to the rest of human society. Body crossings for Dalits was a search for religion to indeed function as a way of life, one that honors their own individual bodies but also gives them a new relationship model for a more elastic social body politic."[12]

Swami Dayananda Saraswati, on the other hand, a prominent Hindu leader and teacher, describes conversion as an act of violence and not as a quest for freedom from violence. In the words of Swami Dayananda,

> Religious conversion by missionary activity remains an act of violence. It is an act of violence because it hurts deeply, not only the other members of the family of the converted, but the entire community that comes to know of it. One is connected to various persons in one's world. The religious person in every individual is the innermost, inasmuch as he or she is connected to a force beyond the empirical. The religious person is connected only to the force beyond he has now accepted. That is the reason why the hurt caused by religion can turn into violence. That is why a religious belief can motivate a missionary to be a martyr. When the hurt of the religious becomes acute, it explodes into violence. Conversion is violence. It generates violence.[13]

These different perceptions of conversion are significant for both communities, since conversion has become the single most important source of tension, controversy and violence between Hindus and Christians in India. It is a combustible issue that ignites passion on both sides, exploding easily into conflicts that lead to death and destruction. Such different memories cause deep suspicion and mistrust, underlying the need for deeper dialogue that aims for mutual understanding and trust.

A Way Forward for Reconciliation

Dialogue on conversion between Hindus and Christian in India is difficult and challenging. This is one of the reasons why such dialogue is not occurring in any sustained and meaningful ways. If reconciliation, truth, mutual understanding, and peace are important concerns of religion and religious communities, then such dialogue is imperative and must be sought actively by both traditions. The following are some of what I regard as necessary for fruitful dialogue and reconciliation on this issue.

I think that the Hindu majority community should take the initiative for this dialogue. Religious traditions need to be especially attentive to the voices of those who experience the tradition as oppressive and unjust, and as denying them power and freedom. Causing suffering to others (*hiṃsā*) and indifference to such suffering are the antithesis of what the Hindu tradition advocates at its highest ethical ideal of non-violence (*ahiṃsā*). Radically different memories of the meaning of the same event, when this event is a source of tension and conflict, must be an urgent incentive for deep dialogue. Dalit Christians, who feel alienated from the tradition and who think that the tradition does not accord them equality, are unlikely to be the initiators of this dialogue.

As noted earlier, there are radically divergent memories and narratives about conversion in both communities. The outcome of such different narratives is a deep mistrust. Dalit Christians, who see the tradition through the eyes of the oppressed, think that Hindu concerns about conversion are disguised efforts to preserve the privileges and power relationships inherent in the hierarchy of caste. Hindus, on the other hand, treat the convert as a child-like individual lured away from community by the seductive and unethical promises of Christian missionaries and who needs to be protected. There is a widespread Hindu suspicion of Christianity as a tradition that is concerned only with increasing its power through conversion; Hindus even have suspicions about the long-term political goals of Christians.

In these circumstances of mutual suspicion about motives, trust is a necessity for dialogue and reconciliation. Such trust will not be easy or immediate and religious leaders have a special responsibility for nurturing its birth and growth. Trust is the source of hope that experiences can be shared and that each religious community can be mindfully attentive to the voices of the other. Trust allows painful memories to be shared, and difficult questions to be asked. Trust enables identification with the others' suffering, and makes possible self-criticism and transformation. The building of such trust is not a single event, but the nurturing of a relationship that cannot be rushed.

My hope is that in the trustful sharing of experiences, truth will emerge. Dialogue cannot be indifferent to truth. Our communities must be willing to receive these truths, however difficult and challenging. Hindu leaders and Hindus will be challenged by the memories of Dalit Christians, to understand the many ways in which they experience the tradition as oppressive and as negating their human dignity and self-worth. This will not be easy since Hindu leaders still come primarily from males of the upper castes who have always experienced power and privilege within the tradition. Having never experienced religiously justified oppression and injustice, they may assume that the tradition that has been good to them is good for all born within it. On the side of Dalit Christians, dialogue could lead to consideration of some of the methods and assumptions of Christian proselytization that cause uneasiness and concern among Hindus. It is an opportunity for Dalits to ask questions about caste and an opportunity for Hindus to speak about those teachings in their tradition that proclaim the equal worth and dignity of all human beings that are not been reflected in social reality and relationships.

Dialogue does not aim for consensus and its success is not to be measured by consensus. It affords a space for mutual sharing and questioning that will hopefully lead to mutual respect, understanding and the experience of our common humanity. Dalits must be allowed to articulate and explain the reasons for their embrace of another tradition; the integrity of such a choice has to be respected and be the basis for meaningful relationships with Hindus. Reconciliation will not occur if Hindus question or deny the rights of Dalits to self-definition.

The sharing of experiences is an important process in the search for understanding, and this becomes particularly important when one group is oppressed by another. We need to understand not only the historical origins of our experiences, but the ways in which the memories of such experiences determine our disposition towards other communities and the mechanisms through which these are transmitted intergenerationally fueling our prejudice, stereotyping and demonizing of other communities. The participation of the other in this process is vital if we are to be honest and not fall into the trap of self-deception. Sharing of experiences in a context like this facilitates our understanding of the other but, just as important, or even more important, our understanding of ourselves. In the mirror of the others' memory, we see ourselves clearly, and especially those features that we prefer not to see. We will not be transformed if we do not open our eyes.

Finally, on the Hindu side, this dialogue must arise from and be sustained by its deepest spiritual wisdom about life's unity. It is from the perspective of life's unity that Hindus can question exploitative and unjust human relationships, which foster conflict and divisiveness, and it is the same perspective which urges us to seek and work for reconciliation and for the quality of human relationships which expresses this central truth of our existence. If our world is indeed a single family, the quality of our relationships should reflect the moral and ethical implications of this truth. We cannot dehumanize another without dehumanizing ourselves; reconciliation with another is also reconciliation with ourselves.

References

1 Mark Juergensmeyer, *Terror in the Mind of God* (Berkeley: University of California Press, 2000), 174.

2 For example, see Juergensmeyer, *Terror in the Mind of God*, 171-178.

3 Rajmohan Gandhi, *Why Gandhi Still Matters* (New Delhi: Aleph Book Company, 2017). See Chapter 7.

4 See Arthur Osborne, *Ramana Maharshi and the Path of Self-Knowledge* (York Beach: Samuel Weiser, 1970), 69.

5 See John Allen Grimes, *Ramana Maharshi: The Crown Jewel of Advaita* (Boulder: Albion Andalus, 2012), 194-95. For other examples, see Chapter 5.

6 *The Ramayana of Valmiki*, trans. Hari Prasad Shastri, 3 vols. (London: Shanti Sadan, 1957-1962), vol.3, 331-332.

7 See "India Literacy," https://www.indexmundi.com/india/literacy.html.

8 See Anantanand Rambachan, "A Hindu Perspective," in *What Men Owe to Women*, eds. John C. Raines and Daniel C. Maguire (Albany: State University of New York Press, 2000), 17-40.

9 For the Christian perspective, I rely on two sources in particular. The first is Thomas Thangaraj, "The Missiological Hermeneutics of a Convert," Exchange, Vol.32, No.1, 37-41, and Sathianathan Clarke, "The Promise of Religious Conversion: Exploring Approaches, Exposing Myths, Exploring Modalities," in *Crossing Religious Borders: Studies on Conversion and Religious Belonging*, eds. Christine Linemann-Perrin and Wolfgang Linemann (Weisbaden: Harrossowitz Verlag, 2012), 590-610. For the Hindu perspective, I rely on Ashok V. Chowgule, *Christianity in India: The Hindutva Perspective* (Mumbai: Hindu Vivek Kendra, 1999). I am grateful to Thomas Thangaraj for his guidance and suggestions.

10 Clarke, "The Promise of Religious Conversion," 602

11 Chowgule, *Christianity in India*, 49-50.

12 Clarke, "The Promise of Religious Conversion," 605.

13 See "Conversion is an Act of Violence," http://www.swamij.com/conversion-violence.htm.

BIBLIOGRAPHY

SELECTED

Primary Sources in English Translation

Bhagavadgītā with the Commentary of Śaṅkarācārya. Translated by Alladi Mahadeva Sastry. Madras: Samata Books, 1977.

Bhagavadgītā. Translated by Winthrop Sargeant. Albany: State University of New York Press, 1993.

Bhagavadgītā. Translated by Swami Dayananda Saraswati. Chennai: Arsha Vidya Centre, 2007.

Brahmasūtra Bhaṣya of Śaṅkarācārya. Translated by Swami Gambhirananda. Calcutta: Advaita Ashrama, 1977.

Bṛhadāraṇyaka Upaniṣad with the Commentary of Śaṅkarācārya. Translated by Swami Madhavananda. Calcutta: Advaita Ashrama, 1975.

Chāndogya Upaniṣad with the Commentary of Śaṅkara. Translated by Ganganatha Jha. Poona: Oriental Book Agency, 1942.

Chāndogya Upaniṣad. Translated by Swami Swahananda. Madras: Sri Ramakrishna Math, 1975.

Eight Upaniṣads with the Commentary of Śaṅkarācārya. Translated by Swami Gambhirananda. 2 vols. *Īśa, Kena, Kaṭha,* and *Taittirīya* in vol. I; *Aitaraya, Muṇḍaka, Māṇḍūkya* and *Kārika* and *Praśna* in vol. II. Calcutta: Advaita Ashrama, 1965-1966.

Śrī Rāmacaritamānasa. Translated by R.C. Prasad. Delhi: Motilal Banarsidass, 1984.

Ramayana of Valmiki. Translated by Hari Prasad Shastri. 3 vols. London: Shanti Sadan, 1957-1962.

Śvetāśvatara Upaniṣad. Translated by Swami Gambhirananda. Calcutta: Advaita Ashrama, 1986.

The Upaniṣads. Edited and Translated by Valerie J. Roebuck. London: Penguin Books, 2003.

Upanishads. Translated by Patrick Olivelle. Oxford: Oxford University Press, 1996.

Secondary Sources

Ambedkar, B. R. *Riddles in Hinduism: The Annotated Critical Selection.* Edited by Kancha Ilaiah. New Delhi: Navayana Publishing, 2016.

Ambedkar, B. R. *Writings and Speeches.* Vol. 3. Compiled by Vasant Moon. Bombay: Education Department, Government of Maharashtra, 1987.

Ambedkar, B. R. *Annihilation of Caste.* Edited and Annotated by S. Anand, with the Introduction of Arundhati Roy. London: Verso Books, 2014.

Andrews, C. F. *What I Owe to Christ.* New York: Abingdgon Press, 1932.

Banerjea, J. N. *The Development of Hindu Iconography.* Delhi: Munshiram Manoharlal, 1974.

Becker, Ernest. *The Denial of Death.* New York: Free Press, 1973.

Borg, Marcus J. *The Heart of Christianity.* New York: HarperCollins, 2003.

Chatterjee, S. and D. Datta. *An Introduction to Indian Philosophy.* Kolkata: Calcutta University Press, 2008.

Chidbhavananda, Swami. *The Bhagavadgita.* Tamil Nadu: Sri Ramakrishna Tapovanam, 1982.

Chinmayananda, Swami. *The Holy Geeta.* Bombay: Central Chinmaya Mission Trust,1995.

Chowgule, V. *Christianity in India: The Hindutva Perspective.* Bombay: Hindu Vivek Kendra, 1999.

Clarke, Clarke. "The Promise of Religious Conversion: Exploring Approaches, Exposing Myths, Exploring Modalities." In *Crossing Religious Borders: Studies on Conversion and Religious Belonging.* Edited by Christine Linemann-Perrin and Wolfgang Linemann. Weisbaden: Harrossowitz Verlag, 2012.

Collett, S. D., ed. *Lectures and Tracts by Keshub Chunder Sen.* London: Strahan, 1870.

Crawford, Cromwell. *Ram Mohan Roy.* New York: Paragon House Publishers, 1987.

Danielou, Alain. *The Hindu Temple*. Translated by Ken Henry. Vermont: Inner Traditions, 2001.

His Eastern and Western Disciples. *The Life of Swami Vivekananda*. 8th ed. Calcutta: Advaita Ashrama, 1974.

Eck, Diana. *Encountering God: A Spiritual Journey from Bozeman to Banaras*. Boston: Beacon Press, 1993.

Eck, Diana. *Darśan: Seeing the Divine Image in India*. Chambersburg: Anima Books, 1981.

Gandhi, M. K. *All Religions are True*. Edited by A. T. Hingorani. Mumbai: Bharatiya Vidya Bhavan, 1962.

Gandhi, M. K. *The Message of Jesus Christ*. Bombay: Bharatiya Vidya Bhavan, 1963.

Gandhi, M. K. *The Voice of Truth*. Ahmedabad: Navajivan, 1969.

Gandhi, M. K. *An Autobiography*. Middlesex: Penguin Books, 1982.

Gandhi, M. K. *All Men Are Brothers*. New York: Continuum, 2001.

Gandhi, M. K. *The Bhagavadgita*. Delhi: Orient Paperbacks N. D.

Gandhi, Rajmohan. *Why Gandhi Still Matters*. New Delhi: Aleph Book Company, 2017.

Goyandka, Jayadayal. *Śrīmadbhagavadgītā Tattvavivekcanī*. Gorakhpur: Gita Press, 2002.

Gracie, David M., ed. *Gandhi and Charlie: The Story of a Friendship*. Massachusetts: Cowley Publications, 1989.

Grimes, Allen John. *Ramana Maharshi : The Crown Jewel of Advaita*. Boulder: Albion Andalus, 2012.

Halbfass, Wilhelm. *India and Europe: An Essay in Understanding*. Albany: State University of New York Press, 1988.

Huyler, Stephen. *Meeting God: Elements of Hindu Devotion*. New Haven: Yale University Press, 1999.

Ilaiah, Kancha. *Why I Am Not a Hindu*. Delhi: Samya, 1996.

Jadhav, Narendra. *Untouchables*. New York: Scribner, 2005.

Jordens, J. T. F. *Dayananda Sarasvati: His Life and Ideas*. Delhi: Oxford University Press, 1978.

Juergensmeyer, Mark. *Terror in the Mind of God*. Berkeley: University of California Press, 2000.

Kimball, Charles. *When Religion Becomes Evil.* San Francisco: HarperOne, 2002.

King, Sallie. *Being Benevolence: The Social Ethics of Engaged Buddhism.* Honolulu: University of Hawaii Press, 2005.

Klostermaier, Klaus. *A Survey of Hinduism.* Albany: State University of New York Press, 1994.

Kopf, David. *The Brahmo Samaj and the Shaping of the Modern Indian Mind.* New Jersey: Princeton University Press, 1979.

Knitter, Paul and Roger Haight. *Jesus and Buddha.* Maryknoll: Orbis Books, 2015.

Knitter, Paul. *Theologies of Religions.* Maryknoll: Orbis Books, 2002.

Lipner, Julius. *Hindus: Their Religious Beliefs and Practices.* London: Routledge, 1994.

Maguire, Daniel C. *A Moral Creed for All Christians.* Minneapolis: Fortress Press, 2005.

Mann, Gurinder Singh, Paul David Numrich & Raymond B. Williams. *Buddhists, Hindus, and Sikhs in America.* New York: Oxford University Press, 2001.

Mukherjee, Prabhati. *Beyond the Four Varnas: The Untouchables in India.* Shimla: Indian Institute of Advanced Study, 1988.

Nirvedananda, Swami. *Hinduism at a Glance.* Calcutta: Ramakrishna Mission, 1979.

Olivelle, Patrick. *Saṃnyāsa Upaniṣads: Hindu Scriptures on Asceticism and Renunciation.* New York: Oxford University Press, 2006.

Osborne, Arthur. *Ramana Maharshi and the Path of Self-Knowledge.* York Beach: Samuel Weiser, 1970.

Patchen, Nancy. *Journey of a Master: Swami Chinmayananda, the Man, the Path, the Teaching.* Fremont: Asian Humanities Press, 1990.

Shriman, Narayan. *The Voice of Truth.* Ahmedabad: The Navajivan Trust, 1969.

Narayanan, Vasudha. "Arcāvātara: On Earth as He is in Heaven." In *Gods of Flesh, Gods of Stone.* Edited by Joanne Punzo Waghorne and Norman Cutler. Chambersburg: Anima Publications,1985.

Prabhupada, A.C. Bhaktivedanta, Swami. *Bhagavadgītā As It Is.* Los Angeles: The Bhaktivedanta Book Trust, 1981.

Prabhavananda, Swami. *The Spiritual Heritage of India*. California: Vedanta Press, 1979.

Radhakrishnan, S. *Bhagavadgītā*. London: Allen and Unwin, 1963.

Rambachan, Anantanand. *The Advaita Worldview: God, World and Humanity*. Albany: State University of New York Press, 2015.

Rambachan, Anantanand. "Global Hinduism: The Hindu Diaspora." In *Contemporary Hinduism*. Edited by Robin Rinehart. Santa Barbara: ABC-CLIO Inc., 2004.

Rambachan, Anantanand. "A Hindu Perspective." In *What Men Owe to Women*. Edited by John C. Raines and Daniel C. Maguire. Albany: State University of New York Press, 2000.

Rambachan, Anantanand. *The Hindu Vision*. Delhi: Motilal Banarsidass, 1992.

Rao, Seshagiri, K. L. *Mahatma Gandhi and C.F. Andrews*. Patiala: Punjabi University, 1969.

Saraswati, Swami Dayananda. *Bhavagad Gītā*. 9 vols. Chennai: Arsha Vidya Research, 2011.

Saraswati, Swami Dayananda. *Light of Truth*. Translated by Chiranjiva Bharadwaja. Delhi: Sarvadeshik Arya Pratinidhi Sabha, 1975.

Sarma, D. S. *The Essence of Hinduism*. Mumbai: Bharatiya Vidya Bhavan, 1971.

Savarkar, V. D. *Hindutva*. New Delhi: Bharti Sahitya Sadan, 1989.

Smith, Huston. *The Religions of Man*. New York: Harper, 1965.

Thangaraj, Thomas. *Relating to People of Other Religions*. Nashville: Abingdon Press,1997.

Thomas, M. M. *The Acknowledged Christ of the Indian Renaissance*. Madras: Christian Literature Society, 1970.

Vivekananda, Swami. *The Complete Works of Swami Vivekananda*. 8 vols. Mayavati Memorial Edition. Calcutta: Advaita Ashrama,1964–1971.

Valmiki, Omprakash. *Joothan*. Translated by Arun Prabha Mukherjee. New York: Columbia University Press, 2003.

Viditatmananda, Swami. *Hindu Dharma*. Ahmedabad: Adhyatma Vidya Mandir, 2008.

INDEX

R

racism 61, 117, 141
Ramana Maharshi 169, 177, 181, 182
Rāmānuja 1, 12, 24, 79, 80, 102, 153
Ram Mohan Roy 4, 66, 77, 95, 98, 107, 180
religion and violence 166
religious difference 92, 124, 125
religious diversity 71, 92, 124
religious evolution 100, 104
renouncer 136, 139
reverence 31, 55, 59, 60, 76, 85, 119, 121, 142, 167
rishi 96

S

Saṁkhya 150
saṁnyāsa 136, 139
saṁsāra 22, 135, 143
Śaṅkara x, 1, 2, 3, 8, 24, 33, 34, 35, 36, 37, 38, 39, 40, 41, 42, 43, 46, 51, 52, 53, 59, 79, 151, 152, 153, 160, 179
satyāgraha 56, 169
Savarkar, Vinayak Damodar 137, 146, 183
Second Vatican Council 131
Sermon on the Mount 67, 121
servant of the poor 117
serving all beings 144
shared identity 5, 113, 115, 117, 166
sharing of wisdom 124
sin 103, 122, 151
smṛti 17, 18, 19
social death 136
spirituality and justice 132
śruti 17, 37
structural injustice 132
Swami Chinmayananda 151, 152, 156, 162, 182
Swami Dayananda Saraswati 80, 93, 152, 156, 162, 174, 179
systemic evil 131

T

theological commitments 4, 88, 117, 124
theology of creation 138
trust 5, 74, 113, 114, 118, 119, 120, 124, 125, 126, 174, 175
Tulasidasa 5, 31, 57, 113, 114, 118, 119, 165, 170

U

untouchability 26, 27, 119, 122, 149, 154, 162
Upaniṣad x, 18, 25, 41, 51, 52, 54, 55, 60, 75, 88, 91, 106, 112, 138, 139, 142, 159, 160, 168, 179

V

varṇas 6, 26, 147, 148, 151, 152
Vedas 2, 8, 16, 17, 18, 26, 33, 34, 37, 39, 41, 42, 44, 45, 46, 48, 60, 80, 88, 138, 148, 149, 173
Vivekananda Swami x, 4, 8, 54, 62, 66, 67, 77, 95, 96, 97, 98, 99, 100, 101, 102, 103, 104, 105, 106, 107, 108, 109, 118, 142, 143, 181, 183

W

world renunciation 99
World's Parliament of Religions 118